GUITAR LESSONS WITH THE GREATS

JOHN ABERCROMBIE · KEVIN EUBANKS
FRANK GAMBALE · SCOTT HENDERSON
STEVE LUKATHER · MIKE STERN

CO-WRITTEN BY MIKE WILLIAMS DEVELOPED BY JOHN XEPOLEAS

EDITED BY ASKOLD BUK
ADDITIONAL EDITING BY EMILY MOOREFIELD AND PAUL SIEGEL
MUSIC ENGRAVING & BOOK DESIGN BY CHELSEA MUSIC ENGRAVING
PHOTOS BY DORIAN ROMER, SUSANA MILLMAN, RICHARD LAIRD,
MARGARET NORTON, LORI STOLL, AND ARMANDO GALLO

PUBLISHED BY MANHATTAN MUSIC, INC.™
© 1994 MANHATTAN MUSIC, INC.

All Rights Controlled and Administered by CPP Media Group.
CPP Media Group and Manhattan Music are divisions of CPP/Belwin, Inc.
All Rights Reserved. International Copyright Secured. Made in U.S.A.

DISTRIBUTED BY
CPP MEDIA
15800 N.W. 48TH AVENUE
MIAMI, FL 33014
(305) 620-1500

Any copying of this material in whole or in part without the express
written permission of CPP/Belwin, Inc., is a violation of copyright law.

Contents

FOREWORD	3
LEGEND OF MUSICAL SYMBOLS	4
JOHN ABERCROMBIE	5
KEVIN EUBANKS	20
FRANK GAMBALE	33
SCOTT HENDERSON	45
STEVE LUKATHER	67
MIKE STERN	82
ABOUT THE CO-AUTHOR	103

CD/Cassette Tracking Info

CD — Cassette Side A

1. INTRODUCTION
2. JOHN ABERCROMBIE EXAMPLE 3
3. KEVIN EUBANKS "EARTH PARTY"
4. FRANK GAMBALE EXAMPLE 1
5. EXAMPLE 2
6. EXAMPLE 3
7. EXAMPLE 4
8. EXAMPLE 5
9. EXAMPLE 6
10. EXAMPLE 7
11. EXAMPLE 8
12. EXAMPLE 9
13. EXAMPLE 10
14. EXAMPLE 11
15. SCOTT HENDERSON MAJOR CHORDS (EXAMPLES 1-4)
16. MAJOR 7♯11 CHORDS (EXAMPLES 5-9)

CD — Cassette Side B

17. MAJOR 7♯5 CHORDS (EXAMPLES 10-12)
18. MINOR 7 CHORDS (EXAMPLES 13-18)
19. MINOR (MAJOR 7) CHORDS (EXAMPLES 19-22)
20. MINOR 7♭5 CHORDS (EXAMPLES 23-27)
21. SUSPENDED CHORDS (EXAMPLES 28-30)
22. PHRYGIAN CHORDS (EXAMPLES 31-34)
23. DOMINANT 7 CHORDS (EXAMPLES 35-37)
24. DOMINANT 7♯11 CHORDS (EXAMPLES 38-41)
25. ALTERED DOMINANT CHORDS (EXAMPLES 42-52)
26. DIMINISHED CHORDS (EXAMPLES 53-54)
27. STEVE LUKATHER/EXAMPLE 14
28. MIKE STERN/EXAMPLE 4
29. EXAMPLE 5

FOREWORD

WHEN JOHN XEPOLEAS CONTACTED ME ABOUT THIS PROJECT, I was excited. Collaborating with six guitarists on an instructional book sounded like a wonderful opportunity. To be able to gather insight directly from artists whom I've long admired was like a dream come true. Although it was difficult to contact them all and work around nonstop recording and touring schedules, dealing with the players themselves couldn't have been easier.

Certain aspects of their playing came as a surprise: for example, the ease with which they played. Artists of this caliber appear to be beyond problems of technique. Furthermore, logic and musicality were always evident. It seemed as if, out of the hundreds of choices in each situation, they always made the perfect choice. Playing standards with John Abercrombie is easy because he intuitively hears the perfect note. Working on a groove pattern with Steve Lukather is simple because he is a master of pop counterpoint. And they are always playing. When I arrived at his place, Mike Stern was playing lines out of Slonimski's *Thesaurus of Scales and Melodic Patterns*. John Abercrombie came to the door with the guitar in his hands.

The content of each lesson was chosen by the artist, and reveals information about each one's thought process as he plays. Kevin Eubanks breaks two of his tunes down into a method, in order to explore ways to play them. Scott Henderson and Frank Gambale present us with new ideas for soloing over various chords. Mike Stern outlines his practice method for soloing. John Abercrombie gives us a glimpse into his harmonic concept.

Putting this book together has provided me with a wealth of information and ideas to work with. I sincerely hope it does the same for you.

I'd like to thank my wife Christine for her never-ending support and encouragement during the past eighteen months as I worked on this book, and thanks to John Xepoleas for involving me. Special thanks to Ronny Schiff for the advice and information. Also thanks to the following for their kind assistance: David Dillon, K.C. Nichols, Christine Martin, Margaret Norton, Dave Olsen, Aaron Stang, Cary Goldberg, and Lori Stoll.

Mike Williams

LEGEND OF MUSICAL SYMBOLS

JOHN ABERCROMBIE

JOHN ABERCROMBIE ATTENDED THE BERKLEE SCHOOL OF MUSIC IN the mid-sixties, along with other soon-to-be-famous jazz artists such as pianist Keith Jarrett. He studied music by day and played at the famed Paul's Mall on Boylston Street at night. Originally a bebopper, John's primary influence was guitarist Jim Hall. Of Hall, Abercrombie says, "Jim's playing had so many pure melodies. His thematic development of ideas was an important influence on me."

While still a student, John landed a gig with gritty blues/jazz organ legend Johnny "Hammond" Smith. "I started working with Johnny while I was still going to Berklee," Abercrombie recalls. "I went to school all day (when I could get up) and played every night." This led to his first album credit, on the Smith trio's 1968 release *Nasty* (Prestige). John's musical development continued in his work with the band Dreams, with Billy Cobham and Michael and Randy Brecker. This group pioneered a form of jazz-rock that came to be known as fusion, and gave John Abercrombie his second recording credit. When he left the band, Abercrombie's replacement was another young innovator: John Scofield.

Jazz drummer Chico Hamilton introduced John to the larger musical worlds of New York and Europe. John joined Hamilton's group in 1970 and played the Montreux Jazz Festival with them in 1970 — his first-ever trip to Europe. Living in New York gave John the opportunity to meet and work with a variety of musicians. His sound and style evolved quickly, prompting a move from the traditional hollow-body jazz guitar to rock instruments and amplification. "Everything was changing," says Abercrombie. "I started playing a solid-body guitar and using distortion."

John released his first "solo" album in 1974, the influential *Timeless* (ECM). With a trio of the same name, including Jan Hammer on organ and Jack DeJohnette on drums, John broke free of the traditional blues and R&B-based organ trios of the '50s and '60s to create a completely new sound.

About the same time, John performed and recorded with Gateway, a trio whose other members were bassist Dave Holland and drummer Jack DeJohnette. The music was a kind of free-form theme-and-variation that developed from the work of Ornette Coleman and was a forerunner of today's harmomelodic funk bands. Gateway released two albums with Abercrombie on guitar, *Gateway* and *Gateway II*.

In the mid-seventies, John led his first band, which included Richie Beirach (piano), George Mraz (bass) and Peter Donald (drums). More recently, in the 1980s the highly-acclaimed John Abercrombie Trio featured drummer Peter Erskine (formerly of Weather Report) and string bassist Marc Johnson (formerly with Bill Evans). The group released a live album, appropriately titled *Abercrombie/Johnson/Erskine* (ECM), that includes stunning interpretations/transformations of such standards as "Alice in Wonderland" and "Stella by Starlight."

With the release of his latest album, *While We're Young*, featuring Dan Wall on Hammond B-3 organ and Adam Nussbaum on drums, John's love for organ trios is well-established. The trio plays an aggressive New York-style contemporary jazz, informed by John's knowledge of and contribution to that corner of the musical world.

Over the last 25 years, John has contributed to more than a hundred albums, including sixteen as a leader. As a sideman, he has recorded with Joe Lovano, McCoy Tyner, Jan Garbarek and Ralph Towner.

John's lessons are based on his concepts of chord melodies, and on new approaches to improvisation.

John Abercrombie

Lesson 1 ▶ Contemporary Chord Melodies

In this lesson, we're going to explore some of the techniques and sounds I use to create my chord melodies. We'll be studying specific voicings for altered dominant chords, the uses of pedal tones, re-harmonization and re-melodizing, and the use of rubato introductions. For the examples in this lesson, I'll be using ideas that can work over a standard tune like "Beautiful Love."

We'll start with chord voicings. I like altered dominant chord voicings that don't necessarily include the third. If you're playing an altered A7 chord, you might play open A, G on the fourth string, C on the third string, and F on the second string (see the third voicing in Example 1). The A is the root, the G is the ♭7, the C is the ♯9, and the F is the ♯5. Note that the third is not included. In the examples that follow, I often use an open A string to help "keep track" of the tonic. Play through these forms.

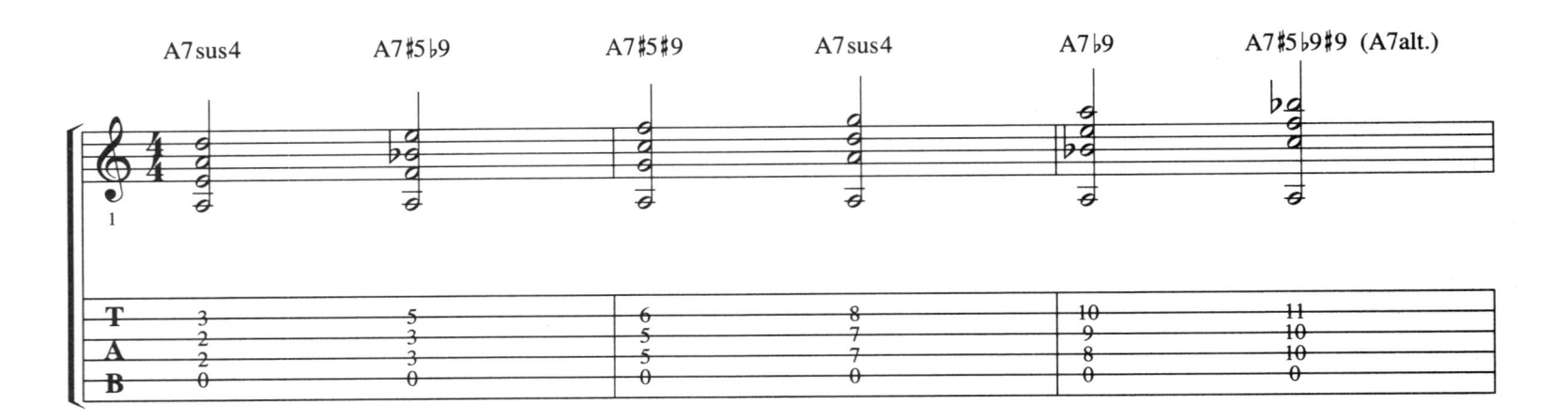

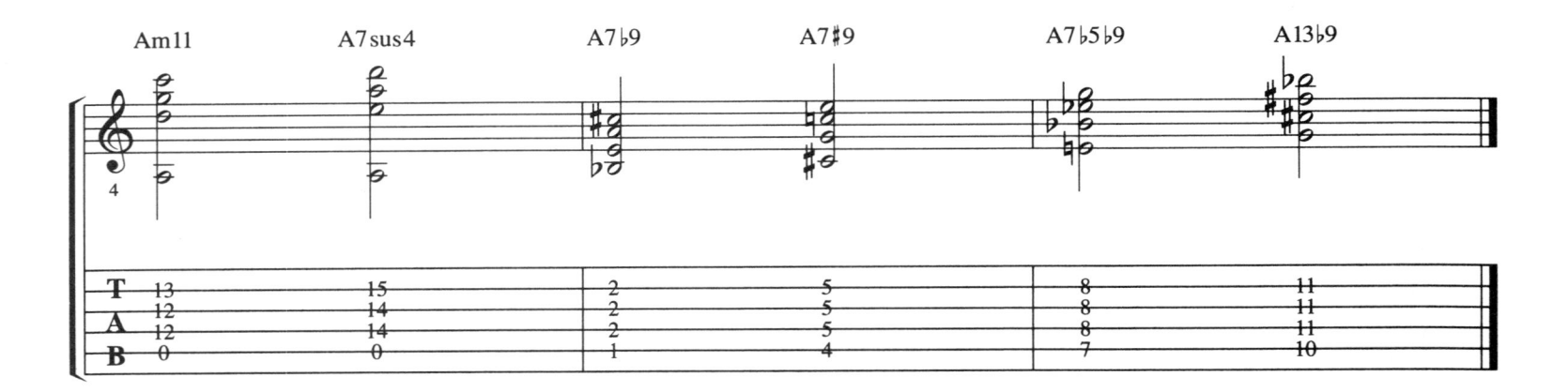

Example 1

JOHN ABERCROMBIE

Try substituting these voicings in common progressions. I think you'll notice a difference: the result is a more "extended" or "modern" sound.

Play Example 2.

EXAMPLE 2

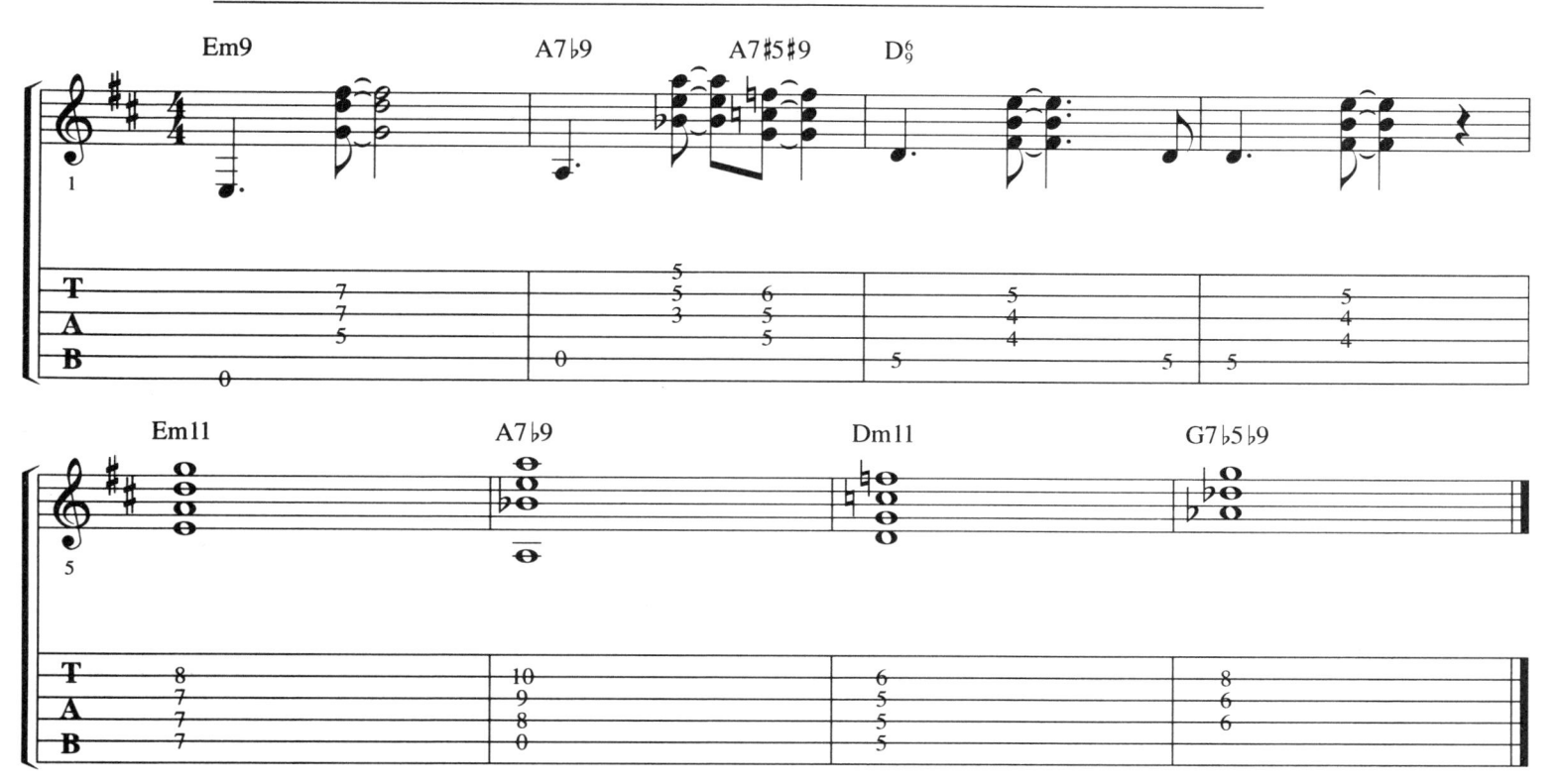

I often start a tune like "Beautiful Love" freely, with no tempo. The following is an example of how I might start this piece. I'm going to base the intro on our altered dominant idea. This song is primarily in the key of D minor, so A7 works well. I'll use the open string as a subtle pedal tone. Try playing Example 3 along with the tape. Remember, when playing "freely," the interpretation is up to you.

EXAMPLE 3

John Abercrombie

John Abercrombie

John Abercrombie

John Abercrombie

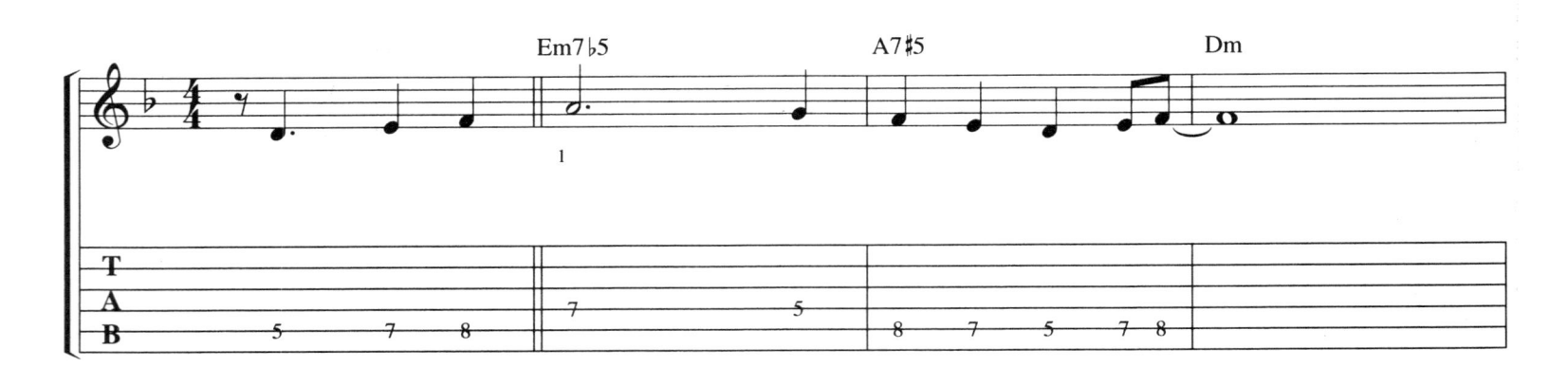

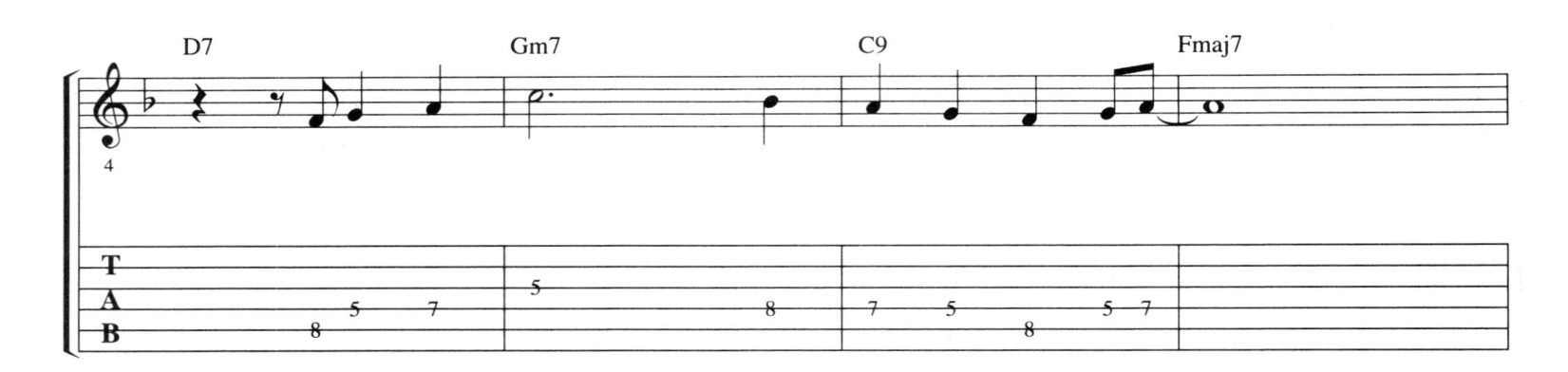

John Abercrombie

Now let's apply the pedal tone concept and the altered dominant chords to the actual tune. Example 4 is the first half of the original melody. You'll need to be familiar with it in order to continue.

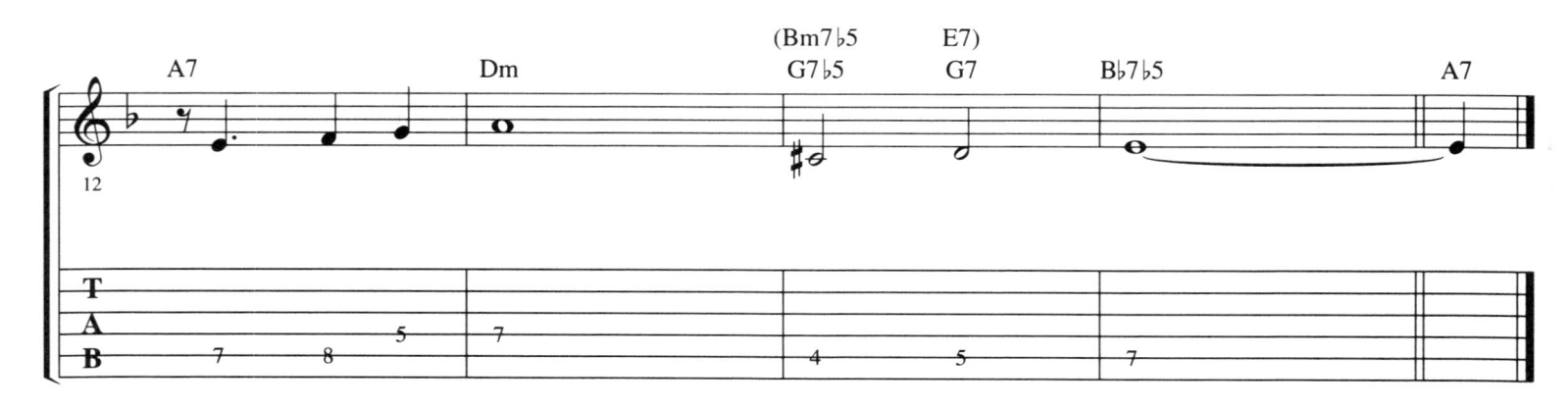

EXAMPLE 4

BEAUTIFUL LOVE
Words and Music by HAVEN GILLESPIE, VICTOR YOUNG, WAYNE KING and EGBERT VAN ALSTYNE
© 1931 WB MUSIC CORP. and HAVEN GILLESPIE MUSIC in the U.S.A. and WB MUSIC CORP. elsewhere throughout the World.
All Rights Reserved   Used by Permission

John Abercrombie

Example 5 is the first half of my version of "Beautiful Love." Play through it, and then I'll discuss the way I approach this song.

Example 5

John Abercrombie

I take liberties with both harmony and melody when playing tunes like "Beautiful Love." Some of the changes that I made are:

1. I used the altered dominant voicings from Example 1 in the first two measures. Although the original chord in measure 1 is *Em7b5,* I'm using an *A7b9* voicing to continue this pedal-tone style.

2. You'll also notice that the A altered dominant harmony continues in measure 2. I play *A7#5#9* as a substitute for A7.

3. Measure 5 is re-harmonized by replacing the Gm7 with *Bbm9/C*. I've also reworked the melody.

4. In measure 6, *C7#9b13* replaces C9. You can find this voicing in Example 1. Notice that it does not include the third.

5. I don't necessarily play the melody in every measure; for example, it does not occur in measures 7 and 8.

I enjoy the sound of two- and three-note chords in this style. It isn't necessary to play five and six-note chords every measure. The *Bbm9/C* is the only five-note chord. I've changed the rhythm of the melody for the most part.

When I play standards, sometimes I don't state the melody until the out chorus (listen to "Stella by Starlight" from *Abercrombie/Erskine/Johnson* on ECM Records). Occasionally I adhere to the true melody, but other times I use the song's form as a vehicle for improvisation from the beginning.

I like to take the sound or shape of a progression and arbitrarily move it into different keys. The last four bars of "Stella by Starlight" are Cm7b5–F7–Bbmaj7–Bbmaj7. I'll substitute *C#m7–F#7–Cm7–F7* for the first two measures. Then I'll start moving it freely through different keys. It doesn't matter if the musicians are together harmonically. There is no way on earth we could be. We're using it as a vehicle to extend an idea — as a theme to improvise freely.

I was heavily influenced pianist Bill Evans. In addition to his harmonic concepts, I studied the way he arranged his tunes. By listening to piano players, you may find approaches and ideas that are different and interesting.

Lesson 2 ▶ Triads Over Bass Lines

When I was working with pianist Richie Beirach, we played a great song of his called "Madagascar." It was a difficult song because it contained harmonic motion that I was not completely familiar with.

Because of the nature of the instrument, very dense-sounding chords can be produced on the piano. To approximate this sound on the guitar, I play triads over bass notes. Acquaint yourself with this sound by playing Examples 6 and 7, which are excerpts from a couple of my tunes.

Example 6

JOHN ABERCROMBIE

EXAMPLE 7

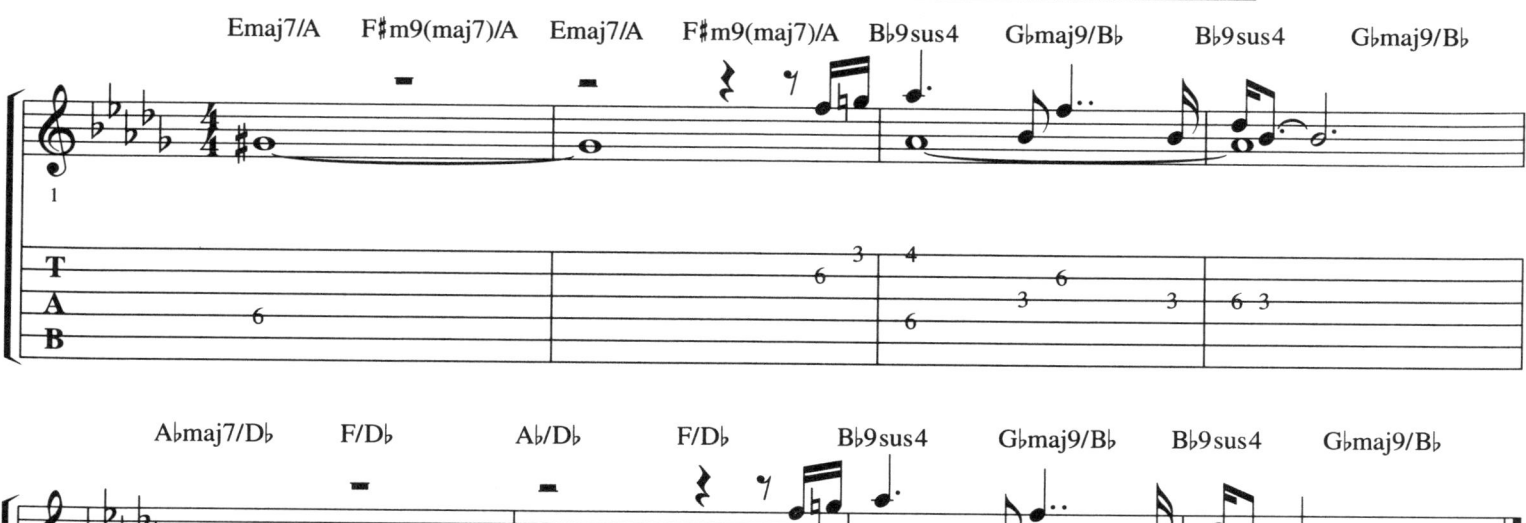

I use these types of chords in my own compositions. Other times I use them as substitute chords in standards. For example, I may re-harmonize an F major chord as an E/F. I could think of this as an *Fmaj7♭5♯9*. Example 8 is a ii7–V7–I7 progression with the E/F substituted for the Fmaj7.

EXAMPLE 8

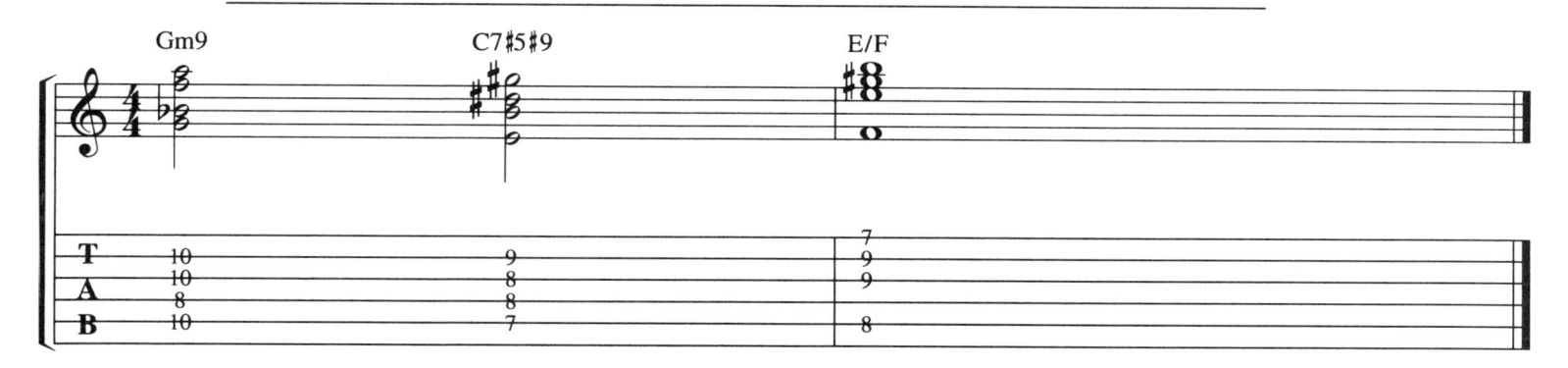

When I solo over this type of chord, I don't think of the scale, but rather the chord, and add the altered notes (see Example 9). The result is an A harmonic minor starting on F.

EXAMPLE 9

Mode 6 of A harmonic minor (A harmonic minor starting on F)

John Abercrombie

In Example 10, I substitute an Aadd9/F for F major. Because I use the open B string, it contains both the #4 and #5.

Example 10

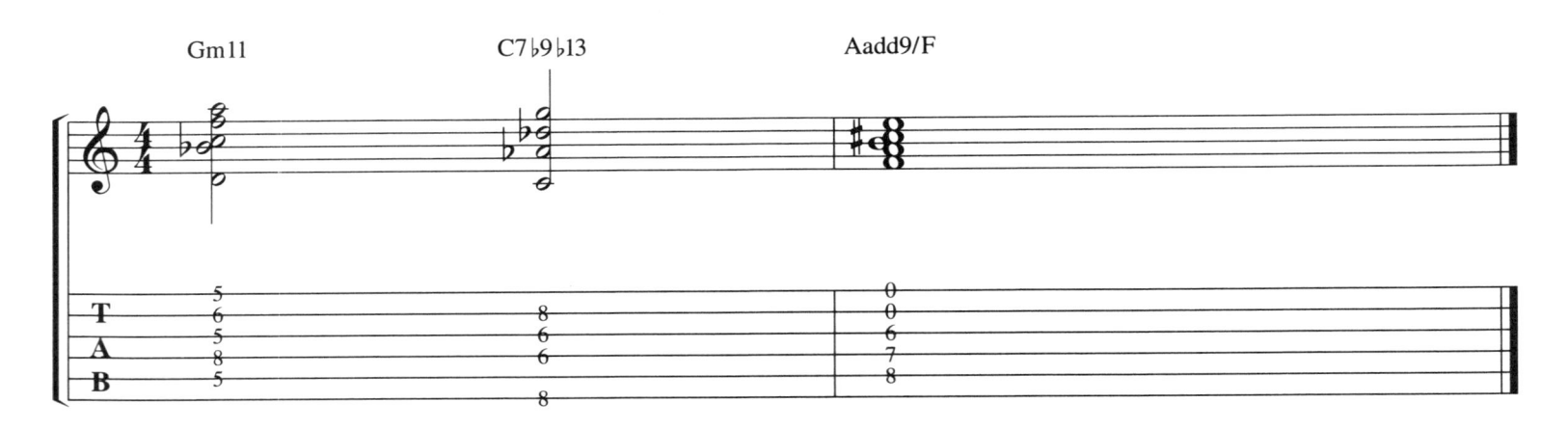

```
      Gm11              C7b9b13            Aadd9/F
```

I use an F Lydian scale with an added #5 over Aadd9/F. If you played it from D, the result would be a D melodic minor. Look at Example 11.

Example 11

Mode 3 of D melodic minor (D melodic minor starting on F)

16

JOHN ABERCROMBIE

LESSON 3 ▶ PURE MELODY

The be-boppers had countless lines and ideas that Charlie Parker (and others) had developed. These melodic figures and concepts became part of the necessary vocabulary for the jazz language. They made use of the information in various combinations to produce interesting solos, rather than studying the style theoretically. The great players of that era — or, for that matter, of every era — possessed a wonderful melodic sense.

I think the best playing employs ear and intuition. Your goal is to combine your knowledge of chords, scales, arpeggios, etc. into your own intuition. *Trust your ear.*

A good exercise for developing your ear, and specifically your melodic sense, is single-string soloing. You'll be finding your way through a sea of chords to find the important notes. Because you won't be playing patterns or scales or riffs, you'll be working towards pure melody. At minimum, you'll find out which notes work best. Example 12 is a solo played on the first string. Record the changes and practice soloing on each string.

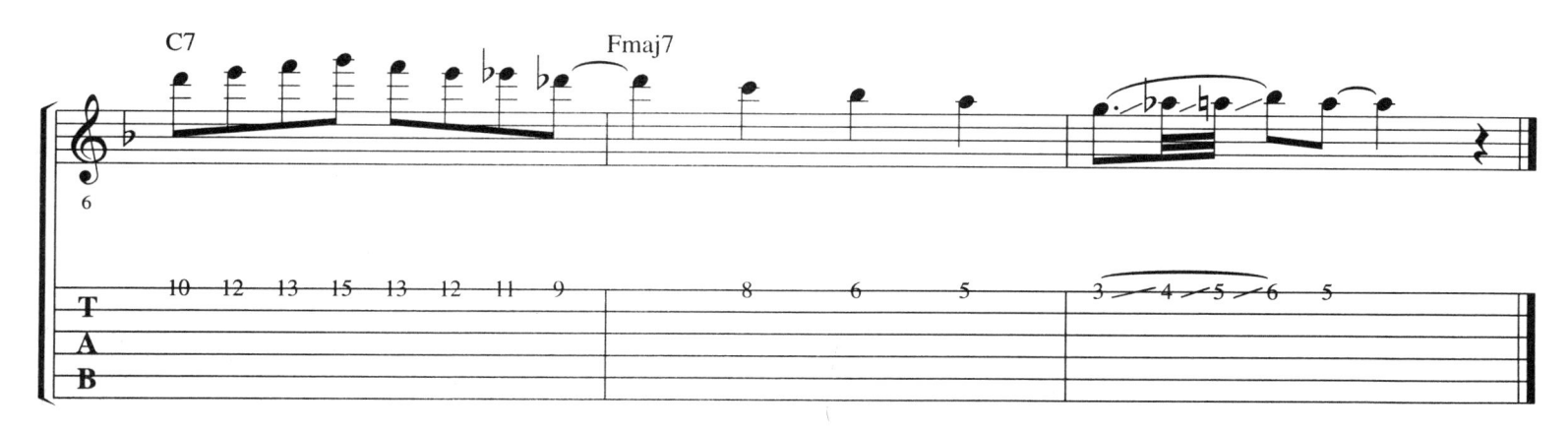

EXAMPLE 12

John Abercrombie

Lesson 4 ▶ Thematic Development

In this lesson, we're going to explore a simple concept to improve thematic development in your soloing. Whatever you play on one chord you can repeat, with a little modification, on another chord. This means that a melodic figure or interval played over one harmony can also be played over a different one, as long as you alter it to fit the new key center. Example 13 illustrates an intervallic/melodic idea that I could use to begin a solo over the changes below.

EXAMPLE 13

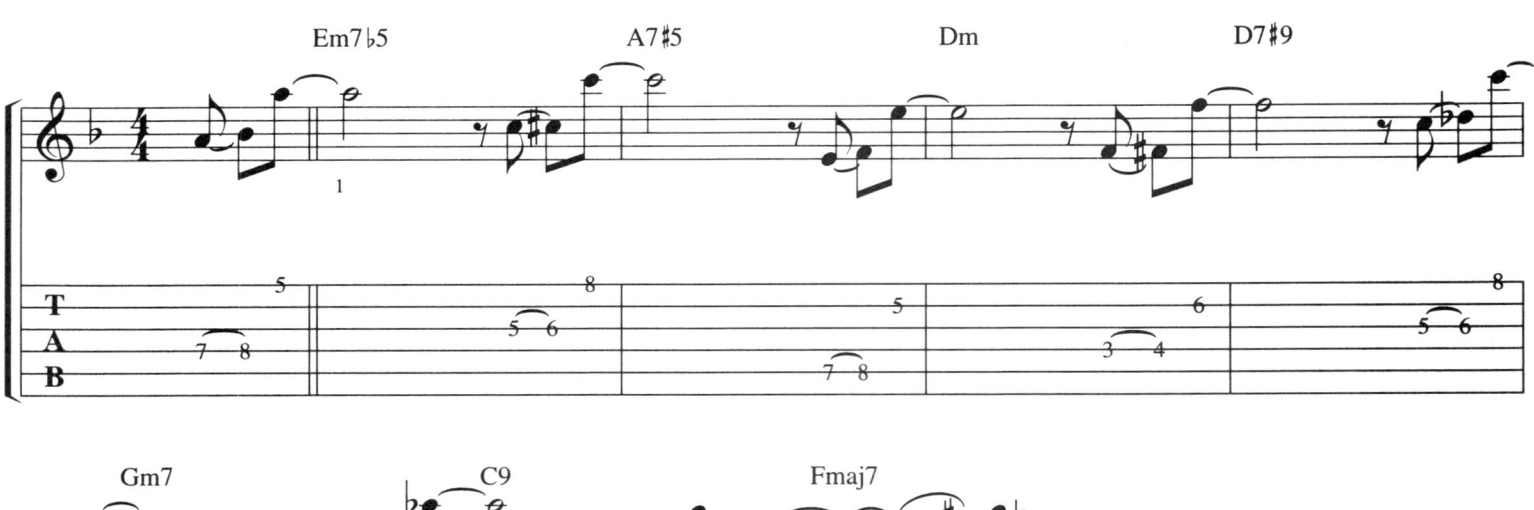

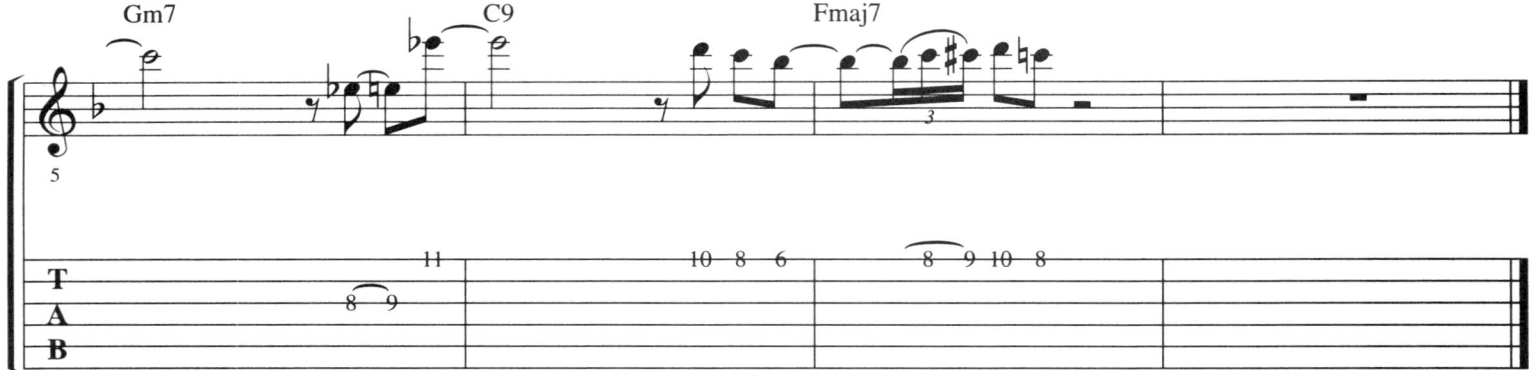

The following themes were derived from the Em7♭5 chord. Using the information provided, alter them to fit the remaining chords in Example 13.

EXAMPLE 14

JOHN ABERCROMBIE

LESSON 5 ▶ MELODIC BASS LINES

This lesson is designed to help you hear through chords and to improve your time. The idea is to solo while limiting yourself rhythmically to half-notes or quarter-notes. I call these melodic bass lines because the pulse is similar to a bass part. You need to think melodically in your choice of notes. You will wind up playing some roots, but you'll also begin "hearing" some other notes that you may prefer. By starting with half-notes, you'll have to make really good choices. This is similar to the single-string solos because it keeps you away from playing patterns. Whenever you put a limit on yourself, you become more aware of the notes you choose.

Play through Example 15 below. The chord changes are common for a jazz standard. You'll notice that alterations and extensions are acceptable in this exercise.

EXAMPLE 15

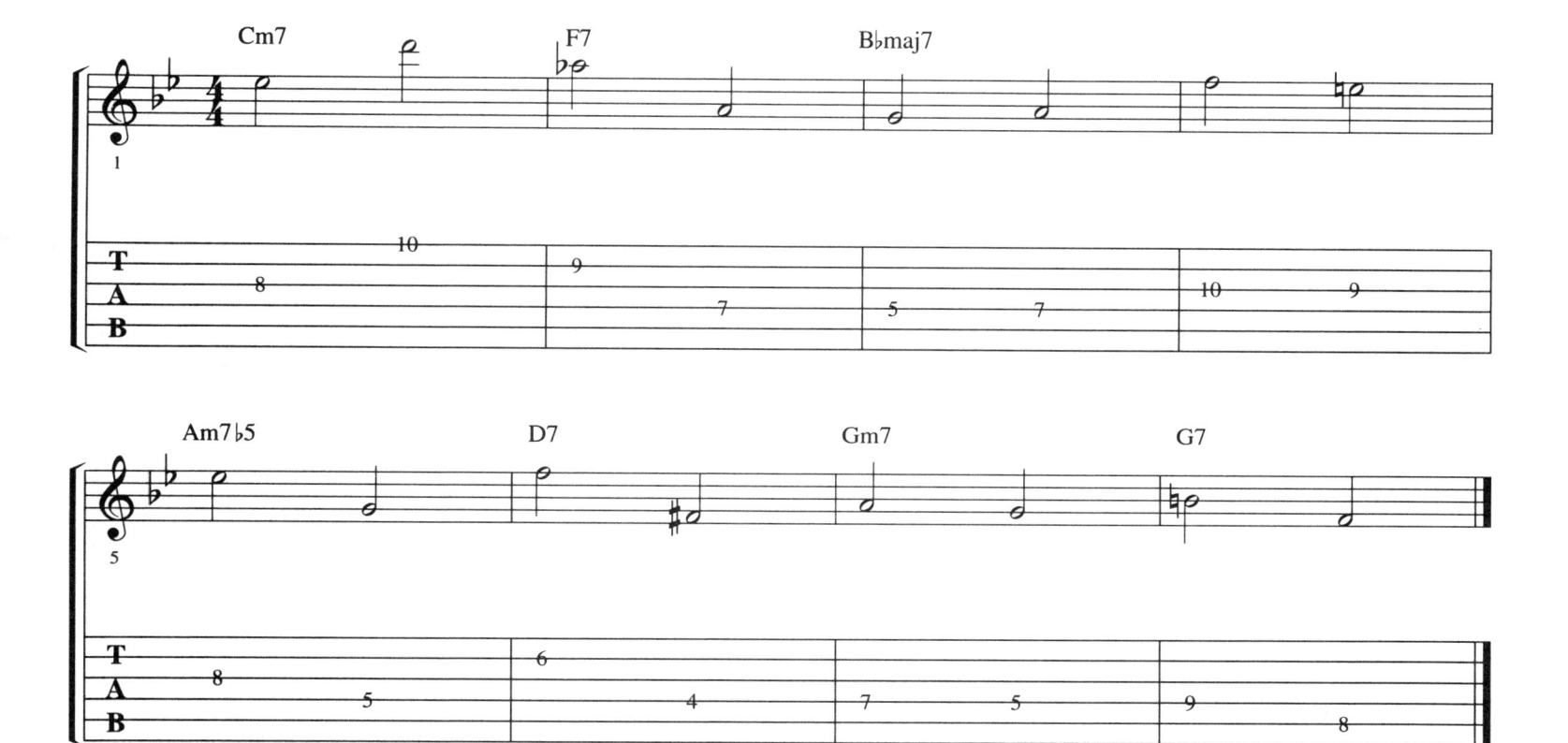

While I've had wonderful experiences playing completely free, I now find greater freedom through structure. In order to get free from chords, you must understand why you got caught in them in the first place.

Kevin Eubanks

A NATIVE OF PHILADELPHIA, GUITARIST KEVIN EUBANKS BEGAN studying violin at age seven. Over the next five years he also became proficient on the piano and trumpet, but finally fell in love with the guitar after seeing James Brown. When his parents turned down his request for guitar lessons, Kevin started teaching himself to play.

Kevin augmented his work in his high school music program by playing in local funk and rock bands. After graduation, he attended the Berklee School of Music in Boston. In 1980, through connections made at Berklee, Kevin auditioned for and joined drummer Art Blakey's band The Jazz Messengers. He appears on the Messengers' 1980 album *Live at Montreux*.

Kevin built his career as a solo artist while keeping a busy schedule as a sideman, recording with Dianne Reeves, Dave Holland, Project G-7 (a Wes Montgomery tribute), and with his brother, trombonist Robin Eubanks. Kevin has also recorded ten albums with his own group, starting with 1983's *Guitarist* (Electra Musician Records). A number of GRP releases followed, including *Sundance*, *Opening Night* (with Branford Marsalis and Buster Williams), *Face to Face* (with Dave Grusin, Marcus Miller and Ron Carter), *Heat of Heat*, *The Searcher* and *Promise of Tomorrow*. His 1988 album *Shadow Prophets* received more radio air play than any other jazz recording of that year. Kevin joined Blue Note Records in 1992 and released *Turning Point* with Marvin "Smitty" Smith and Dave Holland. The composition "Earth Party," which Kevin refers to in his lesson, appears on his latest album, *Spirit Talk*.

Kevin's innovative right-hand technique allows for great harmonic, intervallic and rhythmic freedom and contributes to the unique sound for which he is famous. Although common in classical guitar, counterpoint and polyrhythms are not usually found in jazz guitar work (though they occur more frequently on the piano). Kevin's compositions demonstrate his interest in and facility for odd meters, ostinato rhythms and a new chordal style. Early in his career, Kevin spent a good deal of time transcribing jazz solos; this provided a solid basis later, when his interest in a variety of musical styles led him to examine different harmonic concepts. Although his sound and style is deeply rooted in jazz, it is also easy to trace the influence of well-known players such as Wes Montgomery, John McLaughlin and Jimi Hendrix, whom Kevin counts as major musical influences.

Kevin has enjoyed a long association with renowned saxophonist Branford Marsalis, whom he met at Berklee. With Branford, Kevin has been a member of NBC's *Tonight Show with Jay Leno* band since it was founded in 1992. Accompanying the variety of artists featured on the program serves to showcase Kevin's versatility and vast musical knowledge.

In his lesson, Kevin guides you through two of his more challenging compositions and provides valuable insight into his musical thought processes.

KEVIN EUBANKS

In the brief time that we have together, I'd like to offer you some of my ideas and experiences. I wish it was possible to converse with you and watch as you listen and hopefully react to what I have to say. I admit it feels a little weird to try and "talk" through the pages of a book; it would be better to be in a situation where we could hang, sit down and exchange ideas. But since that's not possible, I'll do my best to communicate what I have to say through these printed words, and trust that the meaning comes across.

Remember, though: there's still two of us here! A book is only a book. It can turn you on, but you've got to give up some energy, too. Bring something to reading this book and you'll probably leave with something positive. In other words, you get back what you put in, so try and work with this book the same way you would work with a live teacher and you'll see good results.

I've structured this section of the book around two original compositions. Each composition is broken down into several lessons, which should be studied bit by bit. I did this so that the examples could be seen and heard in the context of the compositions, not just isolated as technique exercises. This also makes possible a discussion of compositional ideas and how they work.

The first piece, "Earth Party," (from my new Blue Note recording *Spirit Talk*) was inspired by a typical "basement band" jam in the '70s, or what I call the classic "Jam in E." My technique was influenced by some of the bassists I played with growing up. The great Larry Graham created a whole new sound with Sly and the Family Stone. I use my thumb the same way he did, as an "anchor" or main picking digit of the right hand. The bottom note in a voicing is what I refer to as the "bass" note. The thumb can be very funky, if you know how to use it. Many great bass players know all about using their thumbs to produce serious funk, and jazz guitar legend Wes Montgomery used his thumb exclusively.

Let's look at the song from the top. The phrase in second bar can be voiced in one of several ways. I suggest extracting the bass "voice" and playing it as the bass line. Jam on it. Get the feel of it. Mess around with the line and come up with other phrases that feel good; maybe try using chords that accompany the roots. But keep that "basement" feeling — that loose, funky groove — going. Also, pay attention to the meter, which is 9/4. Find phrases that work well in that meter. As you add other notes, you also will see why the bass pattern is so important. The bass part is the cohesive element that keeps this song moving. Throughout the entire piece, your thumb is playing that bass part and acting as the anchor. Remember, it's very important to establish it with authority!

The "folk" sound of bars 16, 17 and 18 reminds me of "Blackbird" by Lennon and McCartney. This section is meant to be more delicate, but keep the bass line pumping.

Those of you who do not use the fingers of your picking hand as individual voices will find parts of this piece impossible to play as written here; but feel free to adapt it to your own particular way of playing. Some technical exercises may help improve your strength and dexterity, and if so, I encourage you to devote time to them. But the most important thing is to find what works for you. Personally, I think that playing with your nose, teeth, or whatever is fine, if you feel good doing it and if you can produce music that way. Don't let any person or school dictate how you execute — if you have a way that works, use it. It's about music, and as long as you use your heart, you can play any way you want and it will touch other people as well as yourself.

Kevin Eubanks

Moving on, the motif of the first two beats of the main phrase (bar 2) returns in bars 39, 42 and 43. (In bars 39 and 43, it is expressed in dominant harmony: *G#7#9* and *B7#9*.) These sections are good ones to practice. Bar 42 outlines the D Lydian and G Lydian harmonies. I suggest going through a harmonic cycle of some kind with this. Try moving it in a cycle of fourths, or perhaps a minor third and a fourth. Use the same motif with different harmony and intervals in harmonic cycles — for example, a dominant seven. You should apply this concept to music or songs you are already familiar with, such as jazz or rock standards. Personally, when I first started to develop this type of phrasing, I would use it over jazz standards. That was one of my ways of digesting new material.

To me, the important sections of this song are in bars 2, 16–18, 42 and 43. If you can master those, the whole thing will come together for you.

A good friend of mine, Ted Dunbar, taught me the importance of the top and bottom notes in a chord voicing. One day, when he was showing me how to conceptualize chord solos, it clicked: my picking hand could be used to express different voices. Of course, playing with the fingers is not new by any means; it is a fundamental element of classical guitar technique. Still, it amazes me how many of the great guitarists of our time — Jimi Hendrix, Led Zeppelin's Jimmy Page, Sly Stone, George Benson, John McLaughlin — who listened to the same music growing up, never really played with their fingers. They use the pick almost exclusively.

I highly recommend learning how to use all four fingers of the picking hand. I have gotten nothing but positive feedback from guitarists who incorporated some finger technique into their playing, or who have discarded the pick altogether. Most guitarists seem to think of finger picking as useful only in mellow-type jazz. Of course, this is nonsense. If you want to know what good finger technique can do, check out blues guitarist Albert Collins or the flamenco guitar work of Paco de Lucia.

As far as my own right-hand finger style is concerned, my thumb plays the downstroke and my index and middle fingers play the upstroke. I don't use fingernails and I do all my practicing on an acoustic guitar. The thumb is very interesting to me — it has strength and presence and power, but also warmth and the subtlety of flesh caressing the string. A broad range of dynamics can be achieved using the thumb.

With regard to chord playing, I use the thumb and three fingers, excluding the fourth finger. This enables me to treat each note as a single voice in the harmony, and to apply concepts such as moving inner voices, contrary motion, etc. If a guitar player only uses a pick, which is not necessarily a bad thing, he or she can only sound a *chord,* so a lot of harmonic subtlety is lost. Imagine a pianist always having to play each note in a voicing at the same time. There would be no harmonic counterpoint — only block chords. It would be rhythmically monotonous, too.

Try playing bars 42 and 43, sustaining each note so that you can hear each individual voice of the chord. In jazz and other forms of contemporary music, when the guitar plays harmony, most of the time it is in block chord form. Personally, I feel that the guitar would be much more effective if the expression of the relationship between two notes did not depend on the use of a pick. I'm talking now about the physical aspect of playing: applying the guitarist's knowledge of harmony and theory to the guitar. Finger picking allows a guitarist more physical contact with the instrument, which in turn leads away *from merely accompanying with chords toward accompanying with harmony.* Fingers orchestrate; it's the difference between touching a pick and touching a note.

In notating this piece I purposely did not use finger or fret markings because I think it's better for you to keep an open mind. Experiment with fingerings; find what works for you. For ease of reading, I have written out this piece in quarter time, but once you become familiar with it, you will hear how it can easily be felt in phrases of eighths. When improvising over this tune, take out the phrases that lean toward the "basement-jam" feeling. Get into the different meters and do your thing. The metronome marking I recommend is ♩=168.

The second song, entitled "Opening Night," was written for guitar and tenor saxophone. It comes from my album *Opening Night* (GRP Records), which features Branford Marsalis (saxophone), my brother David Eubanks (bass), and Marvin "Smitty" Smith (drums).

Although it has a straight-ahead feel, notice again that the meter changes throughout the piece, so it is very important to familiarize yourself with different groupings. In bars 3, 4, and 48, for example, the groupings are in 7. I have put a lot of energy into understanding time signatures, and I feel that this particular composition reflects my interest in jazz and other types of music. I think of it as a very natural integration of different rhythmic ideas.

The harmony outlined in bar 3 is Gm and C, and in bar 4 is A and D. One good exercise might be to continue this same pattern up the neck; also, try different string groupings. Notice the interval leaps and how they resolve; try to create more patterns like these. Also, keep in mind what I said earlier about different voices. The bass line in bars 3 and 4 would be B, C, C♯ and D. Use these two bars as a vamp and do the "basement thing" — I guess for suburban cats I should say the "garage thing" — you know what I mean: just jam on it! What about combining bars 3 and 4 with bar 1 from the first piece? Try the same thing with bars 47 and 48.

Once again, picking with your fingers may be a more natural way of handling this material, but whatever way you play it, I hope it opens up some new possibilities for you.

One idea that I am working with here is melodic rhythm — phrasing. Throughout the piece, you can hear rhythmic resolutions as well as harmonic and melodic ones. The harmonies indicated also outline the rhythmic phrases of the song. Melodic rhythm opens up many possibilities, and it is vital to develop an ear for it. It's not just pitch that's important; rhythm is equally important. Imagine someone speaking in a monotonous voice, with no spaces between their words. Dull, right? That's what playing a stream of notes without any rhythm is like. Remember: *phrasing is conversation.*

Those of you who are familiar with chord solos may find it easy to incorporate the voicings of the melody. In bars 9 and 10, the harmony is $A\flat7\flat9$. The melody, however, can be used on many different types of dominant chords. In bars 24–26, the melody is based on the $B\flat$ *Lydian* scale. Try this pattern over some other major chords.

Because more attention is paid to harmonic or melodic resolution, we have a tendency to think of rhythms as not having natural resolutions, but they do. As you can see, the anticipations of bars 6, 9 and 11 all work together and resolve into bar 15 at letter A. Bars 15 and 17 are working together, as are bars 21 and 23, and the whole first section resolves into bar 27. This creates a "direction" — a feeling that the music is being propelled forward. In the same way, bars 31 and 35 establish the B section. The anticipations of bars 33, 41, 42 and 44 establish a rhythmic continuity. Bars 45 and 46, which set up a "3 feel," build into bars 47 and 48, and then back into the anticipation at bar 50.

In both this piece and "Earth Party," I hope I have made clear to you the importance of rhythmic resolutions as well as melodic and harmonic ones. The guitar is a highly rhythmic instrument and can be effective in many different contexts. After years of study and building technical proficiency, I find that it is more effective to play only what is necessary, instead of everything I am capable of playing — all the scales and sixteenth-notes and emotionally empty patterns which seem to dominate contemporary guitar music.

I am also attracted to musicians who create a *natural* feeling of tension and release, rather than calculating or writing out every melody or solo. A prime example is B.B. King, whose sound and message is identifiable even through a single note. The same could be said for many great musicians — Miles Davis, Thelonious Monk, John Bonham (the late Led Zeppelin drummer), Billie Holiday and many others. This is not to say that musicians such as Coltrane, Oscar Peterson, Steve Vai or John McLaughlin are in any way less musical simply because they tend to play more. It still sounds like they are playing what's necessary because that is what's in their hearts.

Kevin Eubanks

My point is that technique without emotion is ignorant, in music or anything else. Sometimes it seems to me that music schools churn out musicians from a blueprint. Some so-called great musicians find it impossible to play simple chords and melodies. If you can't appreciate a simple musical form, or if you think you're above it, all I can say is good luck trying to express yourself musically.

If you want a high level of technique — by that I mean the ability to play anything you hear in or outside of your head — then my suggestion is to practice and play for many, many hours each day. If you are serious about music, you will reach a point where you are willing to put in this kind of effort, and it will probably continue for several years; and if it ain't a whole lot of fun to do it, then you're in trouble. But regardless of whether music is your life or your hobby, or whether you play fast or slow, remember that it's what's in your *heart* that makes music.

I hope these thoughts have been of some help to you, and that I haven't been too presumptuous in conveying my opinions. Thanks for your time and energy.

Earth Party

EARTH PARTY
Written by KEVIN EUBANKS
© NIVEK PUBLISHING (BMI)
All Rights Reserved   Used by Permission

KEVIN EUBANKS

Kevin Eubanks

Kevin Eubanks

Kevin Eubanks

Kevin Eubanks

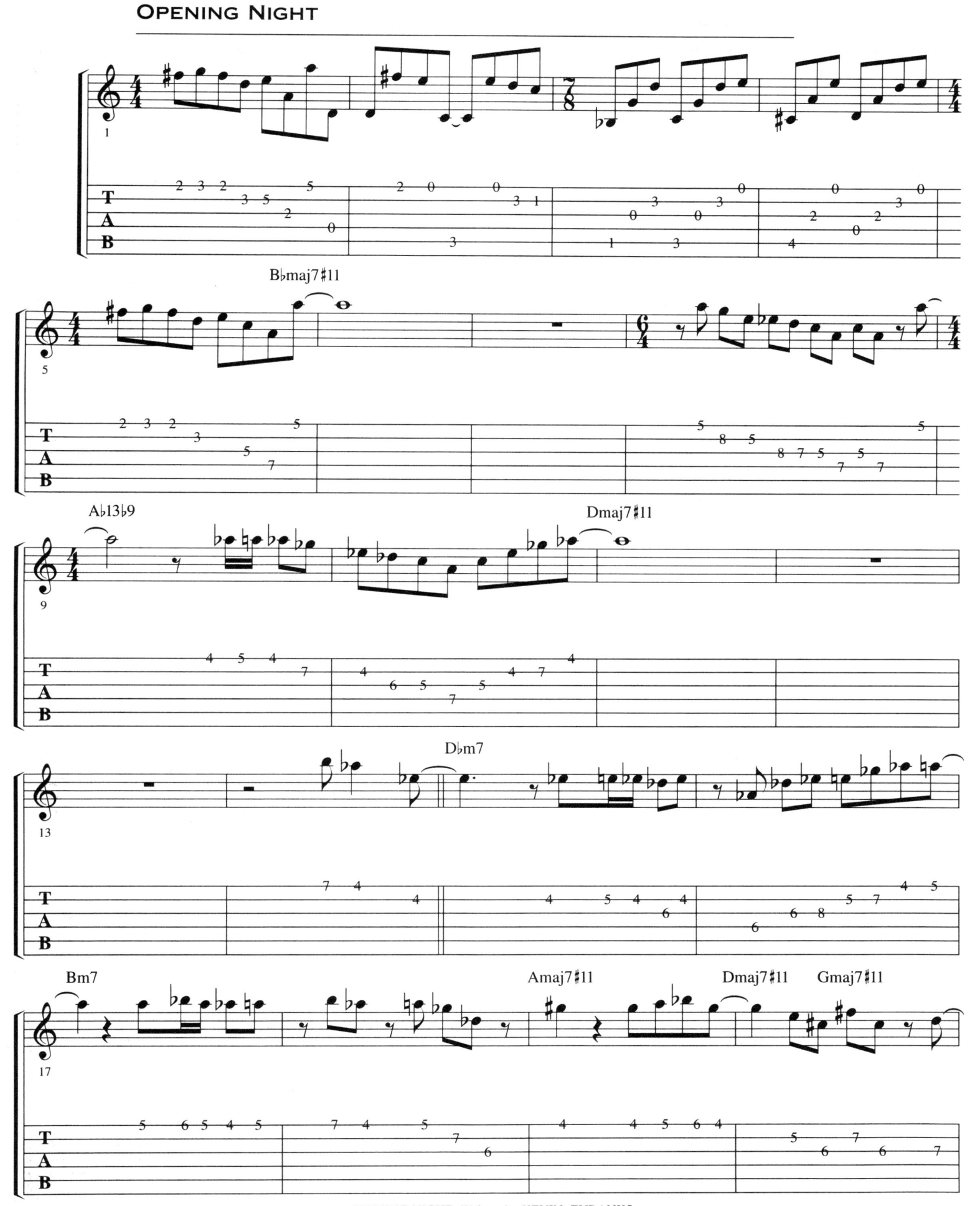

Opening Night

Kevin Eubanks

Kevin Eubanks

Kevin Eubanks

Frank Gambale

Frank Gambale arrived in the U.S. from his native Australia in September 1982 to study at the Guitar Institute of Technology in Hollywood. He graduated as Student of the Year, the school's highest honor. Following graduation, Frank taught at GIT for three years, all the while gigging regularly in Los Angeles with his own group.

In October 1986, Frank joined Chick Corea's Elektric Band. He appears on five of the band's six albums *(Beneath The Mask, Inside Out, Eye of The Beholder, GRP Live,* and *Lightyears)* and has toured throughout the world with them. The group won a Grammy for the song "Lightyears" from the album *GRP Live* in the category "Best Instrumental Group — R&B." Frank has also toured the U.S. with renowned French violinist Jean-Luc Ponty. Frank is currently a member of the acclaimed group Vital Information, along with drummer Steve Smith, keyboardist Tom Coster, and bassist Jeff Andrews. Their latest release is *Easier Done Than Said* (Manhattan/Blue Note/Capitol).

Frank recently released his sixth solo album, *The Great Explorers* (JVC). Backed by Stuart Hamm (bass) and Jonathan Mover (drums), the songs display a hard-edged rock feel that represents a real musical departure for Frank. Also on JVC are his previous solo efforts, *Note Worker* and *Thunder From Down Under.* Frank also released three albums on Legato Records: *Frank Gambale Live, A Present For The Future,* and *Brave New Guitar.*

In both 1989 and 1990, Frank was voted best fusion guitarist in the coveted *Guitar Player* magazine Readers' Poll. He has been on the cover of *Guitar Player* in the United States and many other magazines throughout the world.

Frank continues his work in education via seminars and master classes both in the U.S. and abroad. He recently released a second instructional video for DCI Video, entitled *Modes: No More Mystery,* a follow-up to his critically acclaimed *Monster Licks and Speed Picking* tape. Frank is also the author of three guitar books: *Speed Picking* (published by REH/Hal Leonard), which details his unique sweep-picking style, and *The Technique Book 1* and *2,* covering Frank's unique approach to music theory and improvisation (Manhattan Music Publications).

In his chapter, Frank presents modes as a basis for improvisation in contemporary rock music. He provides us with eleven killer licks in a variety of harmonic settings, which are both challenging and enlightening.

Frank Gambale

In these lessons, we'll take a look at licks which emphasize the ways modes are used in rock, pop, and jazz. One or more modes are present in almost every song you hear. With practice, you can learn to recognize their individual sounds instantly and respond to them immediately.

First we'll look at examples of typical modal chord progressions which you'll probably recognize from music you've heard. I'm going to assume that you already know what a mode is, but I will give you the formula for each mode before I give you the lick.

The most commonly used modes in rock and pop are Dorian, Mixolydian and Ionian (the major scale). I'll begin with examples of each of these; first using them separately, then combining them. Next we'll look at more advanced modes, such as Aeolian, Lydian, Phrygian and Locrian. Then we'll examine the commonly used "jazzier" modes of the melodic minor scale. We'll also talk about the harmonic minor scale.

Without further ado, let's begin.

Lesson 1 ▶ The Dorian Mode

The Dorian is the second mode of a major scale. Therefore, E Dorian is mode 2 of the D major scale.

```
              1  2  3  4  5  6  7
D major  =    D  E  F# G  A  B  C#
E Dorian =       E  F# G  A  B  C# D
```

Compare E Dorian with E major to get the formula:

```
E major  = E  F# G# A  B  C# D# = 1  2  3  4  5  6  7
E Dorian = E  F# G  A  B  C# D  = 1  2  ♭3 4  5  6  ♭7
```

We can see that the 3rd and 7th are lowered in the Dorian scale. Our formula is 1 2 ♭3 4 5 6 ♭7.

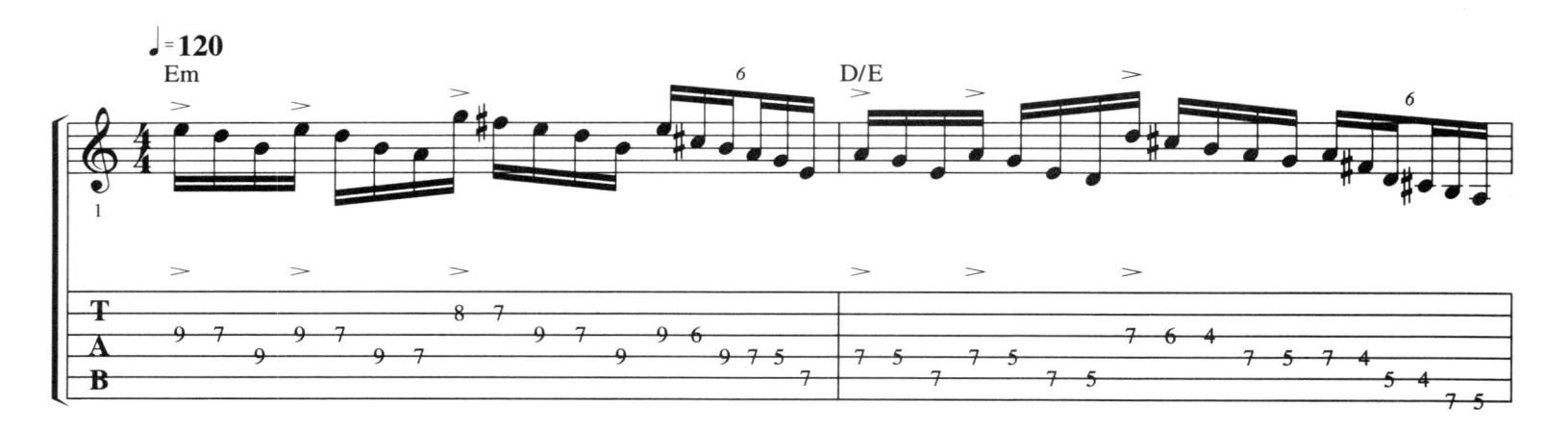

FRANK GAMBALE

LESSON 2 ▶ THE MIXOLYDIAN MODE

The Mixolydian is the fifth mode of the major scale. Therefore, E Mixolydian is mode 5 of A major.

```
                    1   2   3   4   5   6   7
A major      =  A   B   C#  D   E   F#  G#
E Mixolydian =                  E   F#  G#  A   B   C#  D
```

Here is a comparison of E Mixolydian with E major:

```
E major      =  E   F#  G#  A   B   C#  D#  =  1   2   3   4   5   6   7
E Mixolydian =  E   F#  G#  A   B   C#  D   =  1   2   3   4   5   6   b7
```

As you can see, the only difference between E Mixolydian and E major is the lowered 7th.

Frank Gambale

Lesson 3 ▶ The Ionian Mode

Let's look at the Ionian mode over a simple E major chord: E major = E F# G# A B C# D#.

Even though the major scale is very common, I've observed that many guitarists have great difficulty making it sound like rock. This lick will give you some insight into creating a blues/rock effect using the straight major scale (Ionian mode) by extracting a bluesy G# minor pentatonic scale from the notes of the major scale (G# B C# D# F#, or 1 b3 4 5 b7 starting on G#). These notes will be grouped in the lick. See if you can spot them.

FRANK GAMBALE

LESSON 4 ▶ COMBINATION LICK

This lick combines the three modes used so far. It sounds best at a metronome marking of ♩=150 or faster.

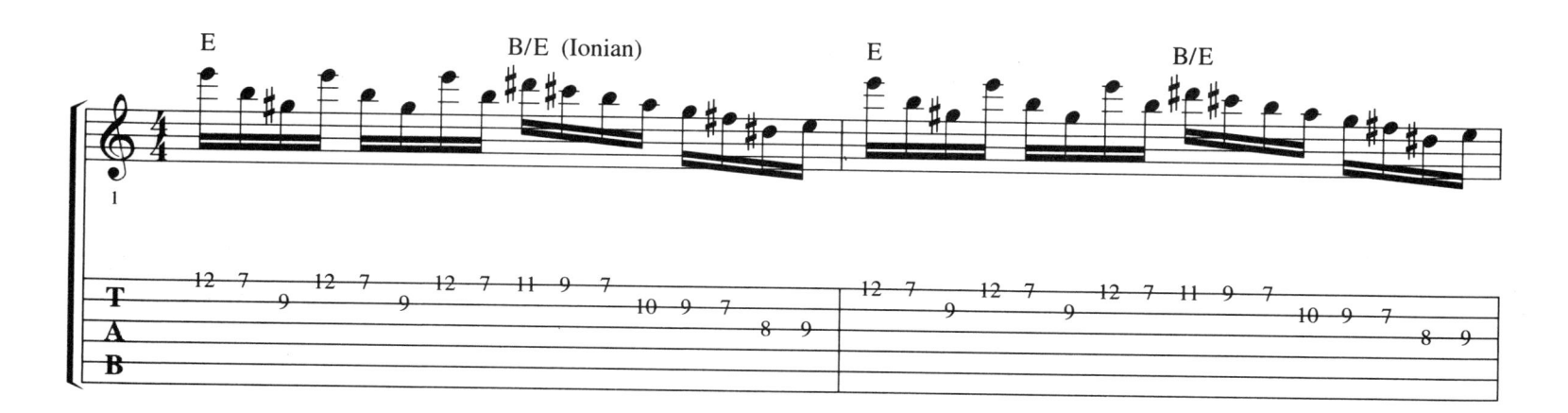

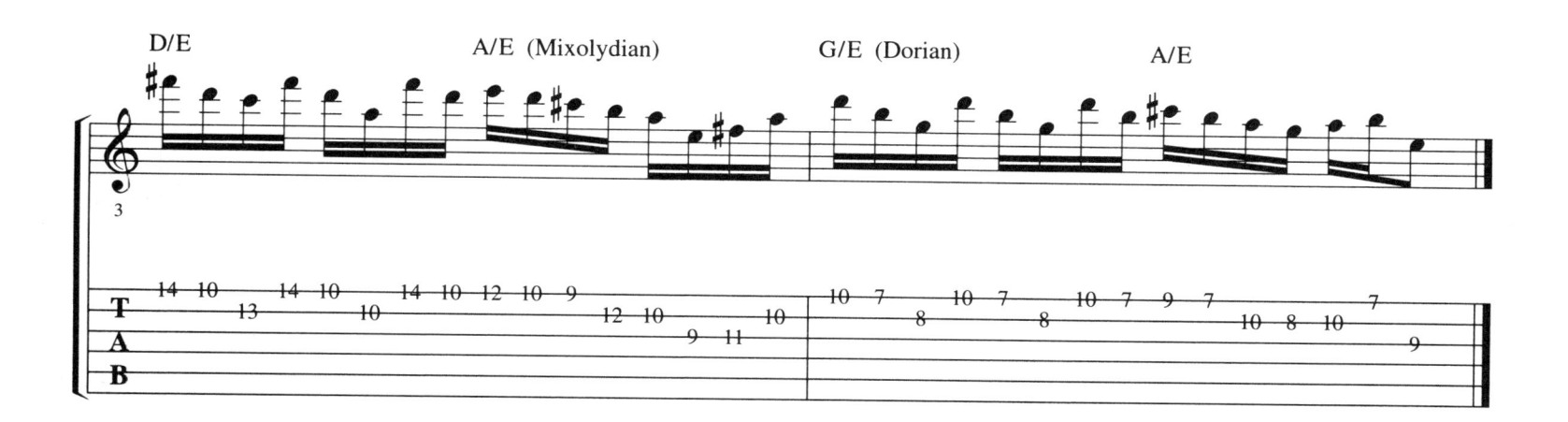

FRANK GAMBALE

LESSON 5 ▶ THE AEOLIAN MODE

Now let's look at the more unusual modes. Here's the Aeolian, which is the sixth mode of the major scale.

```
              1  2  3  4  5  6  7
G major   =   G  A  B  C  D  E  F#
E Aeolian =                  E  F#  G  A  B  C  D
```

Compare E Aeolian to E major to get the Lydian formula:

```
E major   =   E  F#  G#  A  B  C#  D#  =  1  2   3  4  5   6   7
E Aeolian =   E  F#  G   A  B  C   D   =  1  2  b3  4  5  b6  b7
```

Aeolian = 1 2 b3 4 5 b6 b7. Let's look at this mode over an Aeolian progression.

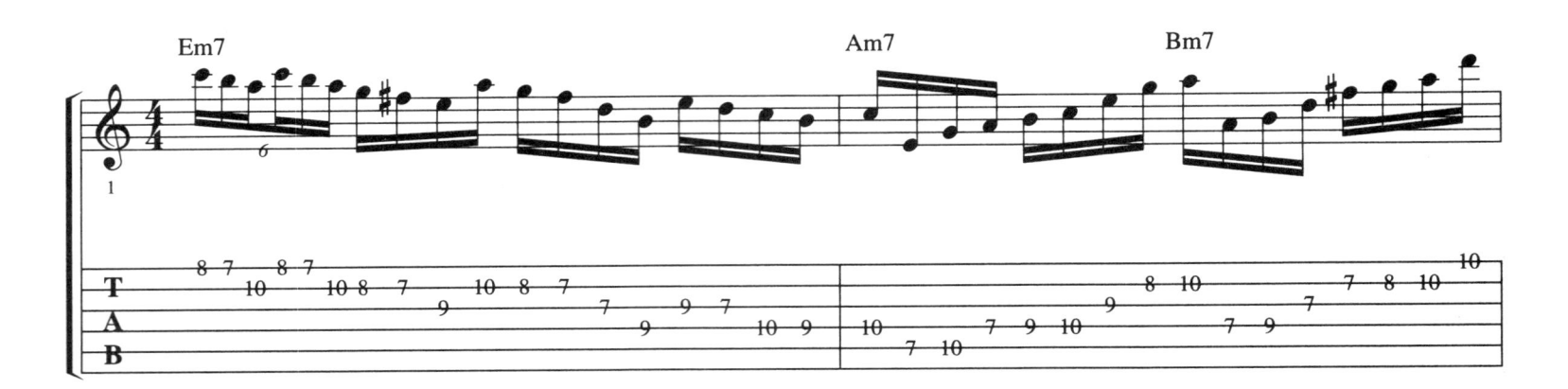

FRANK GAMBALE

LESSON 6 ▶ THE LYDIAN MODE

Lesson 6 is an example of the fourth mode of the major scale, called the Lydian mode. In B major, E Lydian is the fourth mode.

```
              1  2  3  4  5  6  7
B major  =   B  C# D# E  F# G# A#
E Lydian =               E  F# G# A# B  C# D#
```

Compare E Lydian to E major to get the Lydian formula:

```
E major  =  E  F# G# A   B  C# D#  =  1  2  3  4   5  6  7
E Lydian =  E  F# G# A#  B  C# D#  =  1  2  3  #4  5  6  7
```

The only difference between E major and E Lydian is the raised fourth degree. The formula for the Lydian mode is 1 2 3 #4 5 6 7. Lick 6 is played over an E Lydian chord progression.

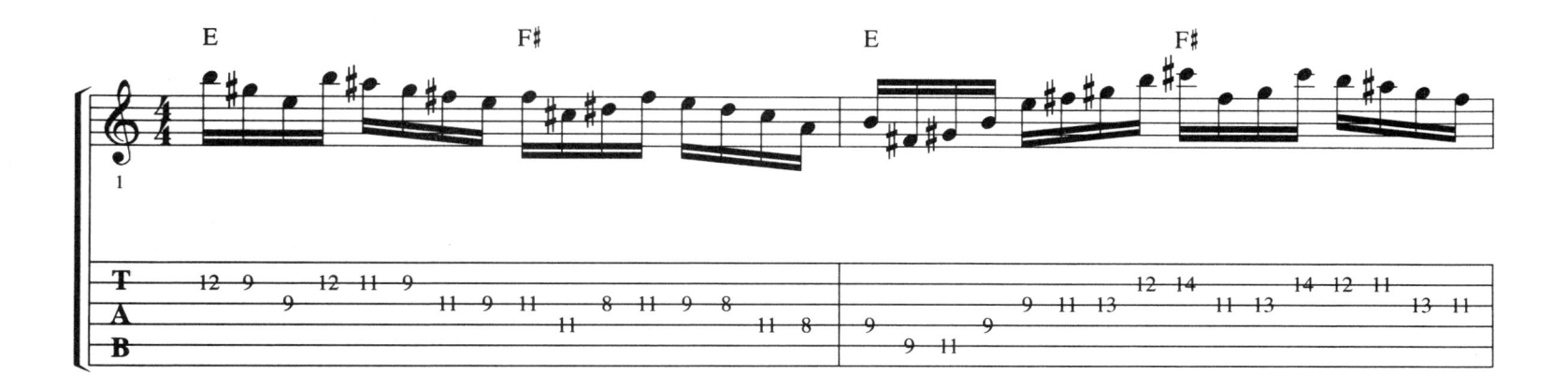

FRANK GAMBALE

LESSON 7 ▶ THE PHRYGIAN MODE

Now let's look at one of the darker, more sinister-sounding modes, the Phrygian. In C major, E Phrygian is the third mode.

```
                  1  2  3  4  5  6  7
C major    =  C  D  E  F  G  A  B
E Phrygian =         E  F  G  A  B  C  D
```

Compare E Phrygian and E major for the Phrygian formula:

```
E major    =  E  F#  G#  A  B  C#  D#  =  1   2   3  4  5   6   7
E Phrygian =  E  F   G   A  B  C   D   =  1  b2  b3  4  5  b6  b7
```

The Phrygian formula is spelled 1 b2 b3 4 5 b6 b7. Lick 7 occurs over a Phrygian progression.

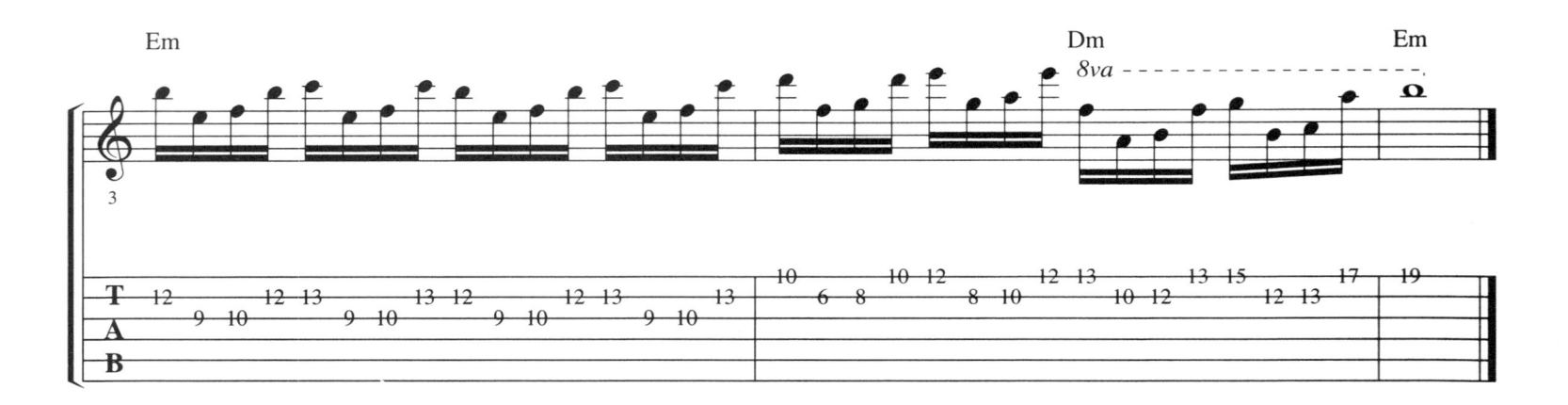

FRANK GAMBALE

LESSON 8 ▶ THE LOCRIAN MODE

Now let's look at the last mode of the major scale, the Locrian mode. This mode is used primarily over minor 7♭5 chords. In F major, Locrian is the 7th mode; therefore F major is equal to E Locrian.

```
                1  2  3  4  5  6  7
F major    =    F  G  A  B♭ C  D  E
E Locrian  =                      E  F  G  A  B♭ C  D
```

Compare E Locrian and E major for the Locrian formula:

```
E major   =  E  F♯ G♯ A  B  C♯ D♯ =  1  2   3   4  5   6   7
E Locrian =  E  F  G  A  B♭ C  D  =  1  ♭2  ♭3  4  ♭5  ♭6  ♭7
```

The Locrian formula is 1 ♭2 ♭3 4 ♭5 ♭6 ♭7. Lick 8 is played over an Em7♭5 chord.

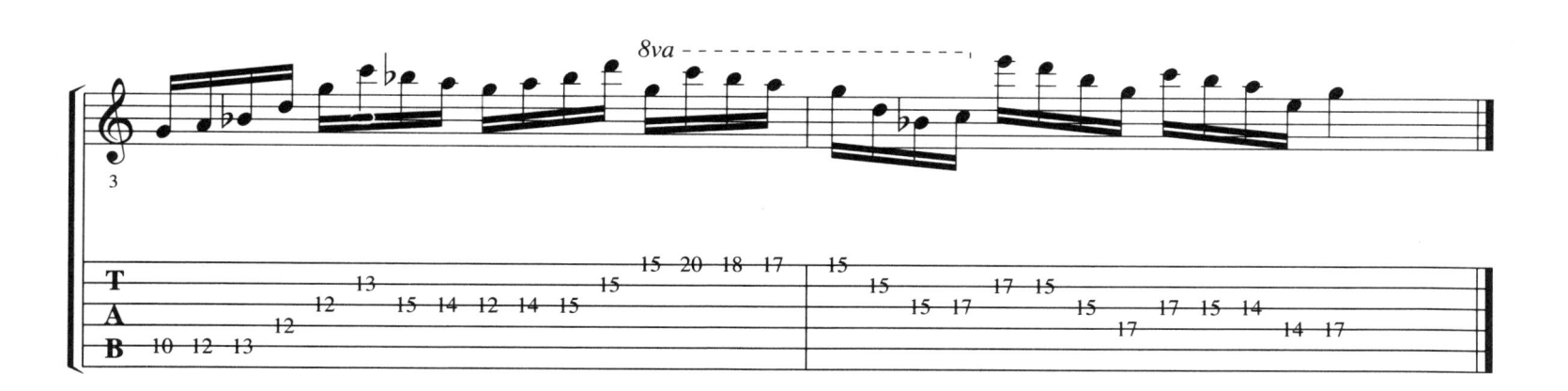

FRANK GAMBALE

LESSON 9 ▶ LYDIAN ♭7

Now it's time to journey into new scale territory! Let's look at the fourth mode of the melodic minor scale, called the Lydian ♭7 scale. Its most common function is to substitute for the Mixolydian mode over dominant chords.

```
                    1   2   3   4   5   6   7
B melodic minor =   B   C♯  D   E   F♯  G♯  A♯
E Lydian ♭7     =               E   F♯  G♯  A♯  B   C♯  D
```

Compare E Lydian ♭7 and E major for the Locrian formula.

```
E major     =  E   F♯  G♯  A   B   C♯  D♯  =  1  2  3   4  5  6  7
E Lydian ♭7 =  E   F♯  G♯  A♯  B   C♯  D   =  1  2  3  ♯4  5  6  ♭7
```

Lydian ♭7 = 1 2 3 ♯4 5 6 ♭7. Lick 9 is E Lydian ♭7 over E9.

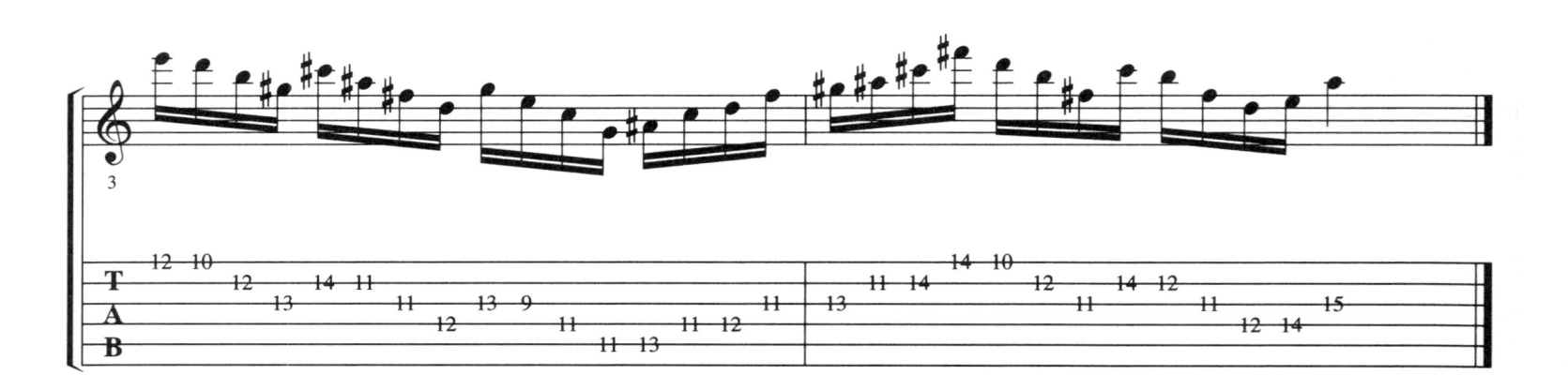

FRANK GAMBALE

LESSON 10 ▶ SUPER LOCRIAN

The next most commonly used melodic minor mode is built on the seventh degree and is called the Super Locrian scale. In F melodic minor, E Super Locrian is mode 7. You can play it over a number of altered 7th chords, including 7♯9, 7♭9, 7♯5♭9, 7♯5♯9, and 7♭5♭9.

```
                   1   2   3   4   5   6   7
F melodic minor  = F   G   A♭  B♭  C   D   E
E Super Locrian  =                 E   F   G   A♭  B♭  C   D
```

Compare E Super Locrian and E major for the Locrian formula:

```
E major         = E   F♯  G♯  A   B   C♯  D♯ =  1   2   3   4   5   6   7
E Super Locrian = E   F   G   G♯  B♭  C   D  =  1  ♭2  ♭3  ♮3  ♭5  ♯5  ♭7
```

The Super Locrian formula is 1 ♭2 ♭3 ♮3 ♭5 ♯5 ♭7. Lick 10 is E Super Locrian played over E7♯9.

FRANK GAMBALE

LESSON 11 ▶ PHRYGIAN MAJOR

The last mode we'll look at is the harmonic minor 5th, which is commonly used over 7♭9 chords. This is called the Phrygian major mode. The A harmonic minor is the same as E Phrygian major.

```
                        1  2  3  4  5  6  7
A harmonic minor  =  A  B  C  D  E  F  G♯
E Phrygian major  =              E  F  G♯ A  B  C  D
```

Compare E Phrygian major and E major for the Locrian formula:

```
E major          =  E  F♯ G♯ A  B  C♯ D♯ =  1  2  3  4  5  6  7
E Phrygian major =  E  F  G♯ A  B  C  D  =  1 ♭2  3  4  5 ♭6 ♭7
```

The formula for Phrygian major is 1 ♭2 3 4 5 ♭6 ♭7. Lick 11 is E Phrygian major played over E7♭9.

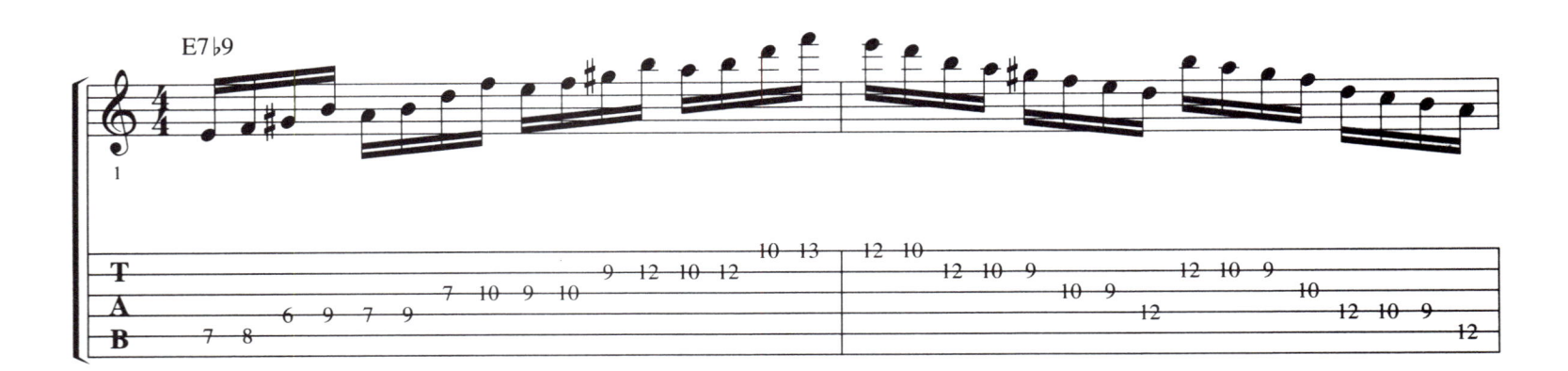

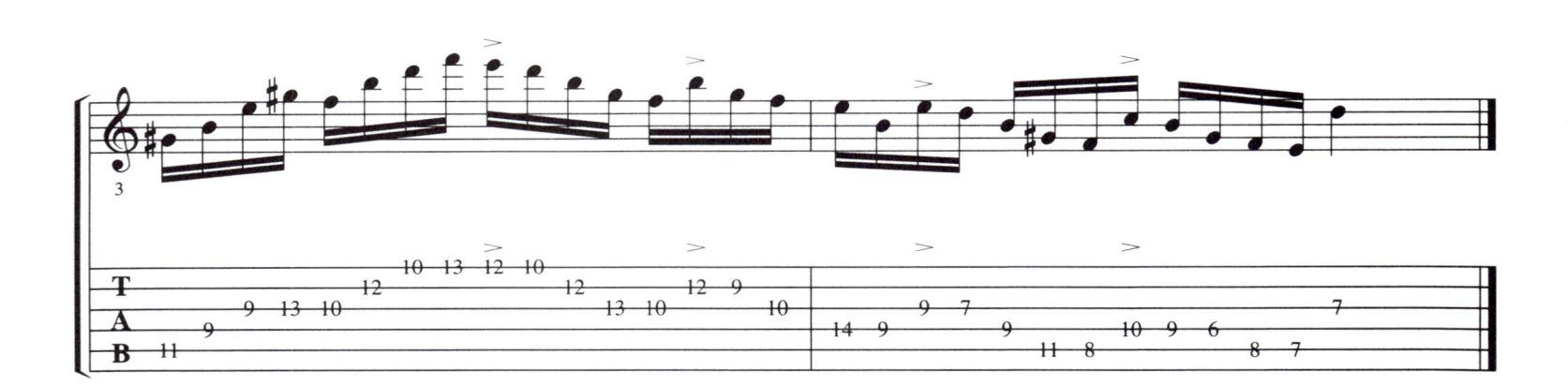

SCOTT HENDERSON

BORN IN 1954, SCOTT HENDERSON GREW UP IN AN ERA WHEN rock 'n' roll dominated popular music and guitarists dominated rock 'n' roll. Henderson was influenced by Jimmy Page, Jeff Beck, Jimi Hendrix, Ritchie Blackmore, and the great blues guitarists Albert King, Albert Collins, and Buddy Guy. Although he considers himself a blues-rock player, Henderson was inspired by jazz and the Mahavishnu Orchestra to create the improvisational style for which he is now known.

"A lot of the jazz I heard in high school just sounded like a blur of notes to me," says Henderson. "It didn't hold my attention. Then I heard Miles and Wayne Shorter and knew these guys had the sense not to play a million notes and have the next guy come up and do the same thing. To me, the great bands have a sense of space and melody in their music, as well as a sense of adventure."

Henderson's own sense of adventure led him from Florida Atlantic University to Los Angeles. Since 1982 he has played with Chick Corea (in the first Elektric Band), Jean-Luc Ponty, bassist Jeff Berlin's group Players, and Weather Report's Joe Zawinul.

Currently, Henderson and bassist Gary Willis co-lead the critically acclaimed Tribal Tech, which recently released its sixth album, "Face First" (Bluemoon Records). In some ways, Tribal Tech personifies Henderson's "dream band," and his rock, jazz, and blues-inflected playing and composing have brought praise from both jazz and rock circles. Constant touring keeps Tribal Tech in the forefront of new music and Scott Henderson on the cutting edge of modern playing. He was named Best Jazz Guitarist by *Guitar World* magazine in 1991, and also came in first in *Guitar Player's* 1992 Reader's Poll.

Scott is a member of the faculty of Musician's Institute in Hollywood and has written columns for *Guitar World* and *Guitar School* magazines. He is the author of *The Scott Henderson Guitar Book*, a collection of his compositions (available from Hal Leonard Publishing) and has released two instructional videos on REH, "Jazz Fusion Improvisation" and "Melodic Phrasing."

In his chapter, Scott reviews common chord types with an eye to soloing options. The 54 examples provide valuable insight into his style of improvisation.

SCOTT HENDERSON

"What do I play over this chord?" I hear that question a lot, but it's a hard one to answer quickly because usually there are many choices. In this chapter we'll look at the most common chord types and explore the soloing choices.

The basic tools of improvisation are chord tones with arpeggios, scales, and chromatic passing notes. Most solos combine all of these. A good solo also incorporates good rhythmic and melodic phrasing, which is not easy to teach in a book (my video *Melodic Phrasing* on REH might be more helpful in that area). Transcription is also very important, because the tools described in this chapter are merely "words," and when you transcribe, you see these words used in musical sentences. A major scale as presented here may not sound like much; but in the hands of a great player using hip phrasing and a few chromatic passing notes, a major scale can be awesome! So it's very important not to just learn the words, but to learn how good players use them, and learn from that as well.

Let's start. First, I'll give you the chord type, then we'll look at a list of choices. Each choice will have an explanation, and a musical example. To make it easier, all chord types will have C as the root.

EXAMPLE 1 — MAJOR SCALE (ALSO CALLED THE IONIAN MODE)

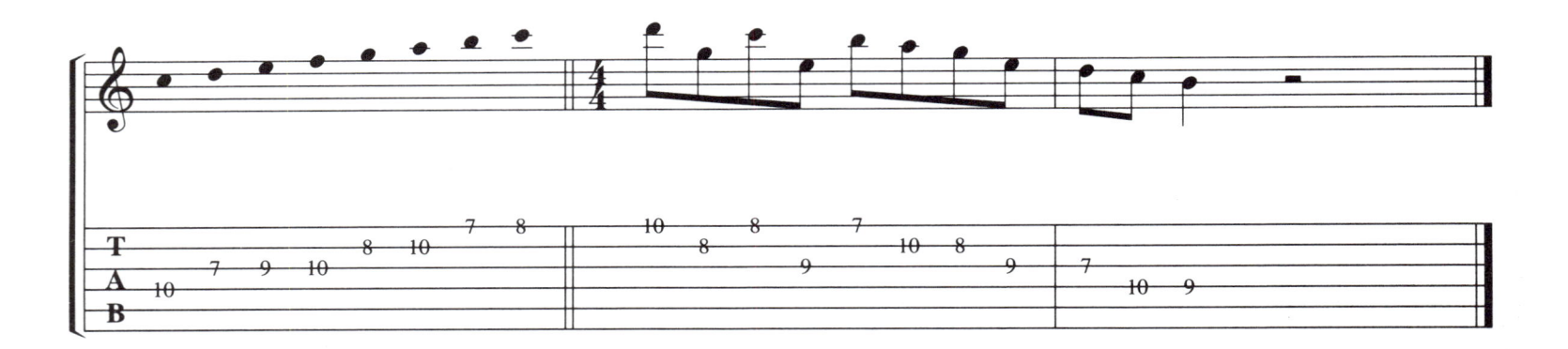

EXAMPLE 2 — MAJOR 7 ARPEGGIO

I usually include the ninth in this arpeggio. You should learn to play it in all five positions.

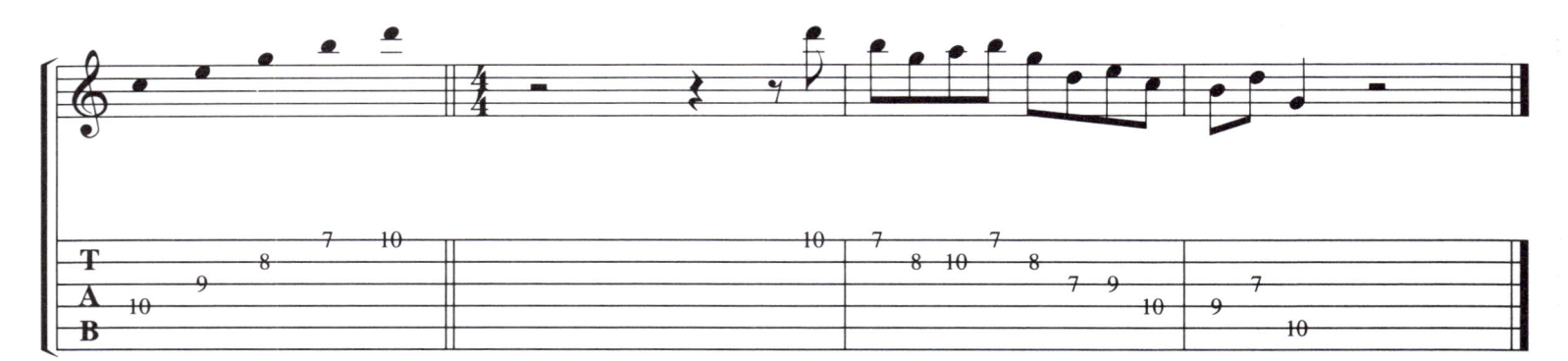

SCOTT HENDERSON

EXAMPLE 3 — MAJOR TRIADS ON 1, 4, AND 5

The major triads C, F, and G all contain notes from the C major scale. The major triad is a very strong sound and a great improvisational tool. Over a Cmaj7, the G triad creates the 5th, 7th, and 9th. The F triad, like the F in the major scale, is better in passing. It creates the 4th, 6th, and root.

EXAMPLE 4 — MINOR PENTATONIC SCALES ON 2, 3, AND 6

Because I've played a lot of blues, I see the pentatonic scale as minor. These three pentatonic scales all contain notes from the C major scale. Over Cmaj7, the D minor pentatonic scale gives a C6/9 sound. Be careful: this scale has a passing F. The E minor pentatonic scale creates a Cmaj13 sound. Carlos Santana has used this really well. The A minor pentatonic scale is a bit "country" sounding. Technically, the A minor pentatonic scale played over Cmaj7 would be called C major pentatonic, but I call it the "Allman Brothers scale."

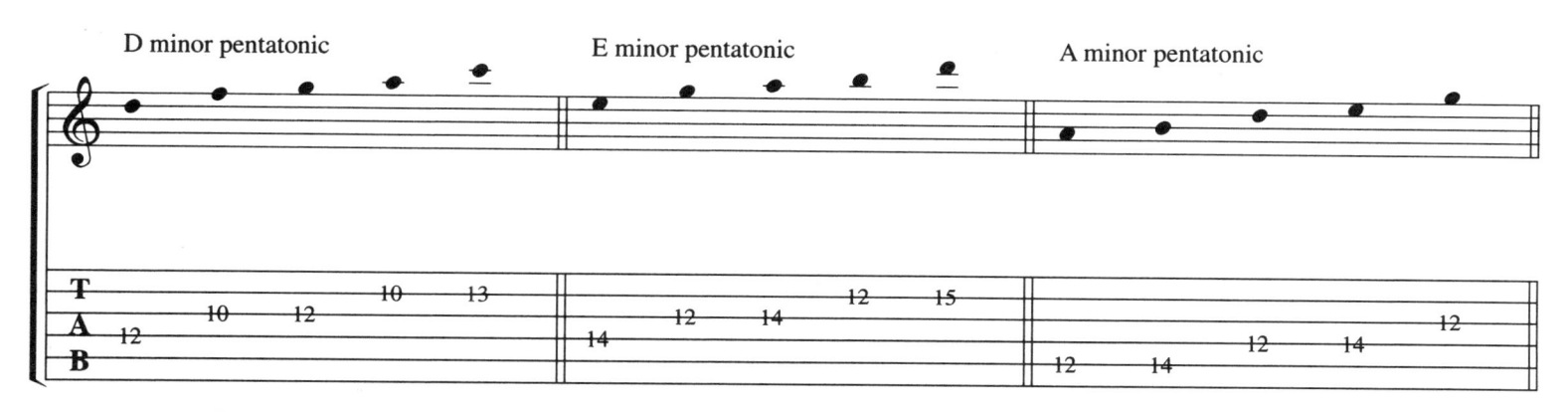

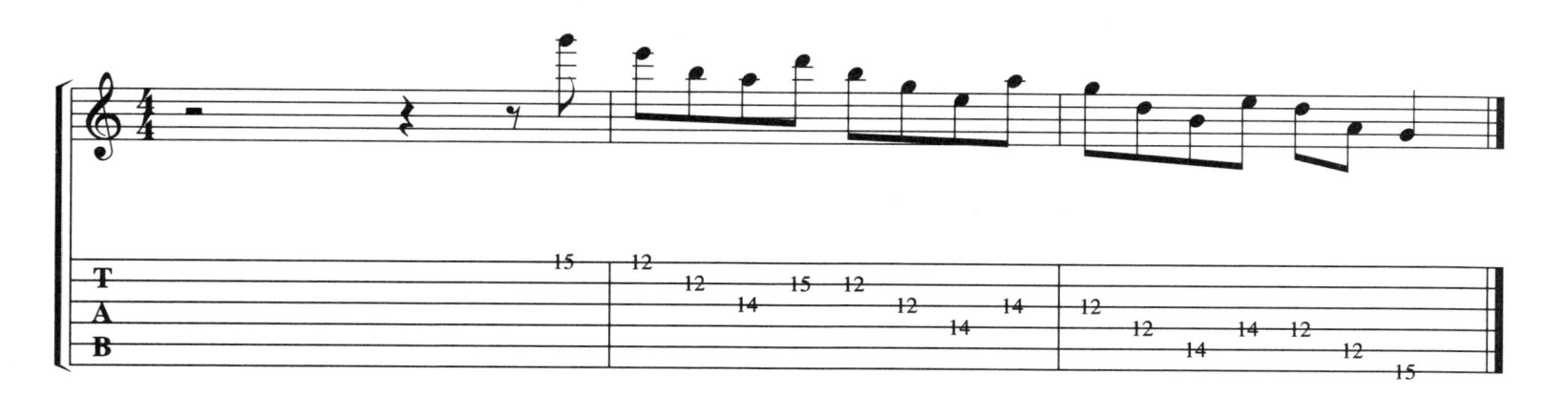

SCOTT HENDERSON

The following ideas will give you sounds that are common extensions on major 7 chords.

EXAMPLE 5 — LYDIAN MODE

This is simply a major scale up a fifth. Over Cmaj7, play the G major scale. You're now playing the C Lydian mode. The 7th of the G major scale (F#) is the #11 of the Cmaj7 chord.

EXAMPLE 6 — MAJOR 7 ARPEGGIO UP A 5TH

This works the same way the Lydian mode does. By playing a Gmaj7 arpeggio over Cmaj7, you create a Cmaj7#11 sound.

*Chromatic passing tone

EXAMPLE 7 — MINOR PENTATONIC ON 7

The B minor pentatonic scale contains notes from the G major scale, which is the C Lydian mode. For you blues players, we now have four minor pentatonic scales to play over Cmaj7: Bm, Am, Dm, and Em. Try your blues licks in all four. Some will work better than others, but you'll eventually learn which licks sound best in each scale.

SCOTT HENDERSON

EXAMPLE 8 — MAJOR TRIAD ON 2

A D major triad over C gives the sound of C6/9#11. Composers commonly use the chord symbol D/C, meaning a D triad over a C bass, to create the 6/9#11 sound. The simple, open sound of a triad sometimes sounds more modern than a full voicing (and D/C is faster to write than C6/9#11).

EXAMPLE 9 — MINOR 7♭5 ARPEGGIO ON ♭5

Playing the G♭m7♭5 arpeggio over Cmaj7 is another way to get a 6#11 sound. The m7♭5 arpeggio is not one of my personal favorites, but I've found a few good uses for it.

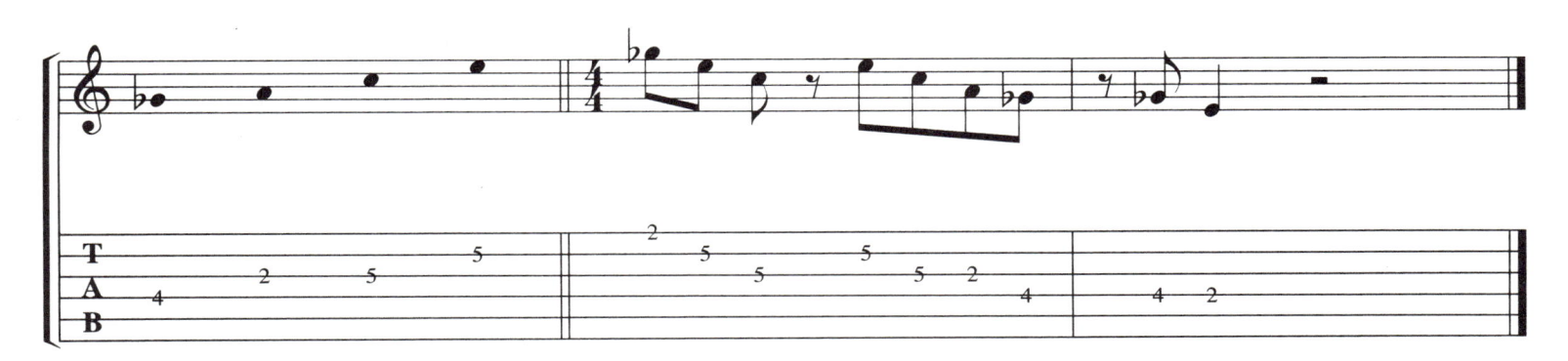

The maj7#5 chord functions differently than the maj7 chord. Adding a 6, 9, or #11 to a maj7 extends the chord, but raising the 5th creates an entirely new chord type. The following ideas can be played over a Cmaj7#5, or they can be used over a Cmaj7 chord to create tension.

EXAMPLE 10 — MELODIC MINOR SCALE ON 6

This scale is called the Lydian augmented. If the chord is Cmaj7#5, you would play an A melodic minor scale. This is one of the modes of the melodic minor scale. You'll see more of these modes later.

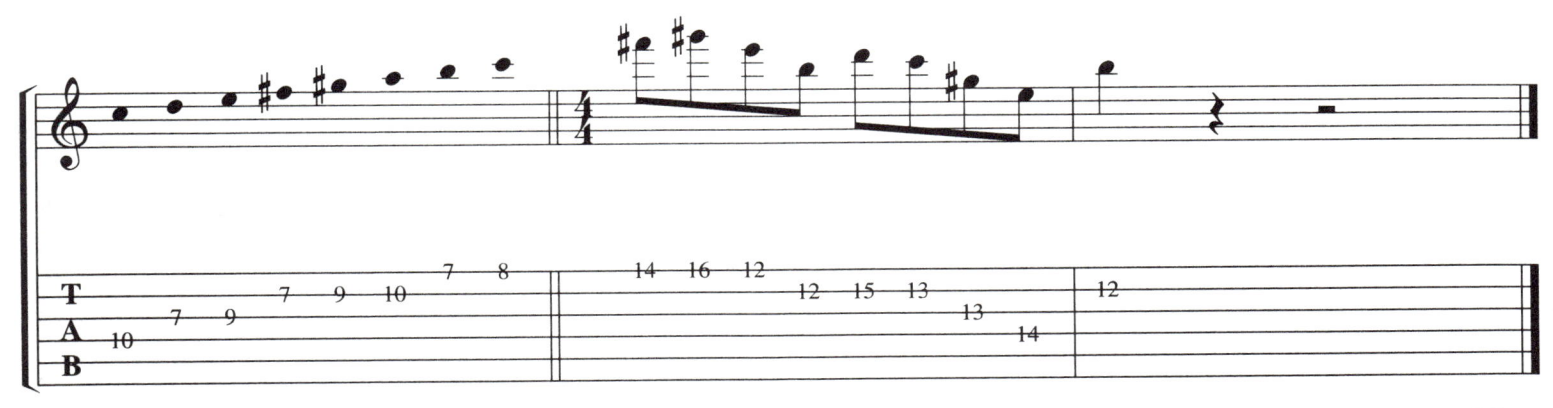

SCOTT HENDERSON

EXAMPLE 11 — MINOR 9 (MAJOR 7) ARPEGGIO ON 6

This is simply a melodic minor scale without the 4th and 6th. Anytime you can use the melodic minor scale you can use this arpeggio. It's written three positions below.

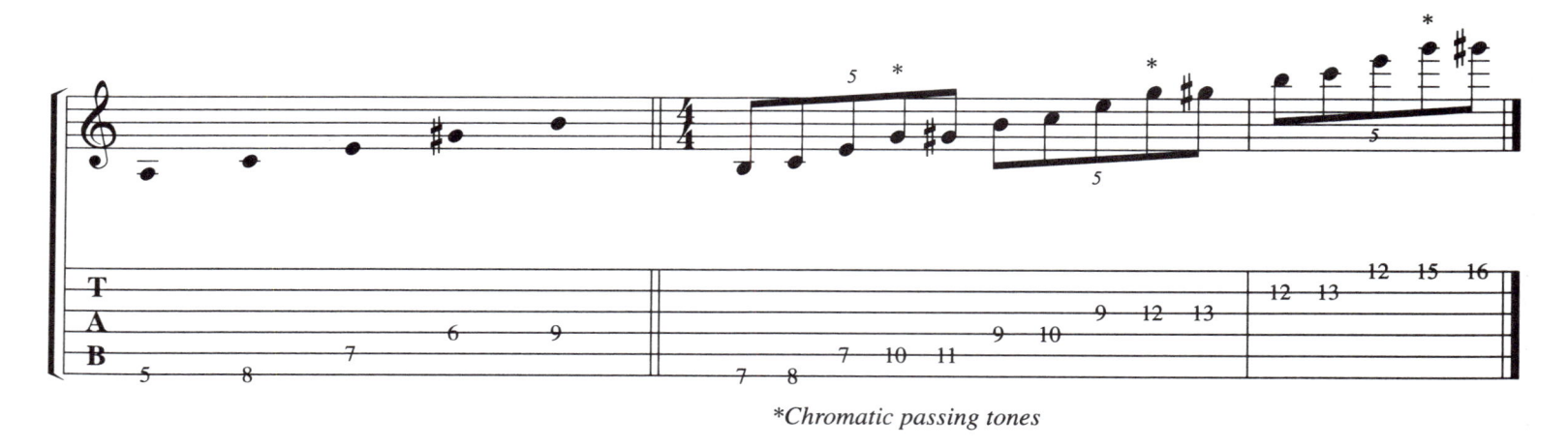

*Chromatic passing tones

EXAMPLE 12 — MAJOR TRIAD ON 3

As you can see from the chord diagram of Cmaj7#5 this chord is simply an E triad over a C root, so playing the notes of an E triad will define the chord perfectly. Many times you would see this written as E/C.

The following ideas can be played over a Cm7 chord.

EXAMPLE 13 — DORIAN MODE

This is simply a major scale down a whole step, in this case B♭ major. This is the scale that's usually played over minor 7.

▶ 50

SCOTT HENDERSON

EXAMPLE 14 — AEOLIAN MODE (NATURAL MINOR)

Playing an E♭ major scale over a Cm7 gives you the C Aeolian mode. It's the same as Dorian except that it has a ♭6 (A♭) instead of a ♮6 (A). It's a little darker-sounding than Dorian.

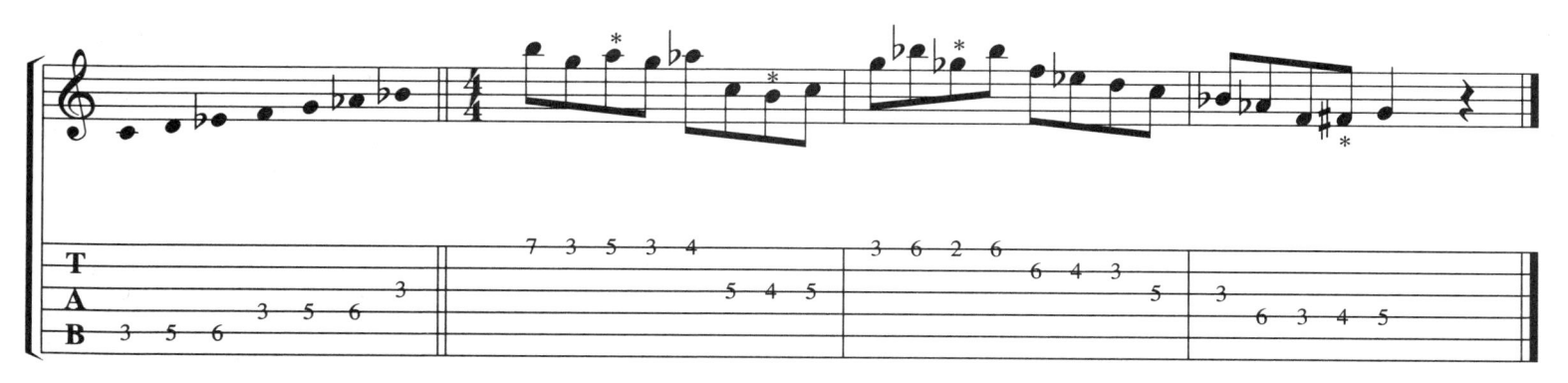

*Chromatic passing tones

EXAMPLE 15 — MAJOR 7 ARPEGGIO ON ♭3

An E♭maj7 arpeggio will give you the sound of Cm9.

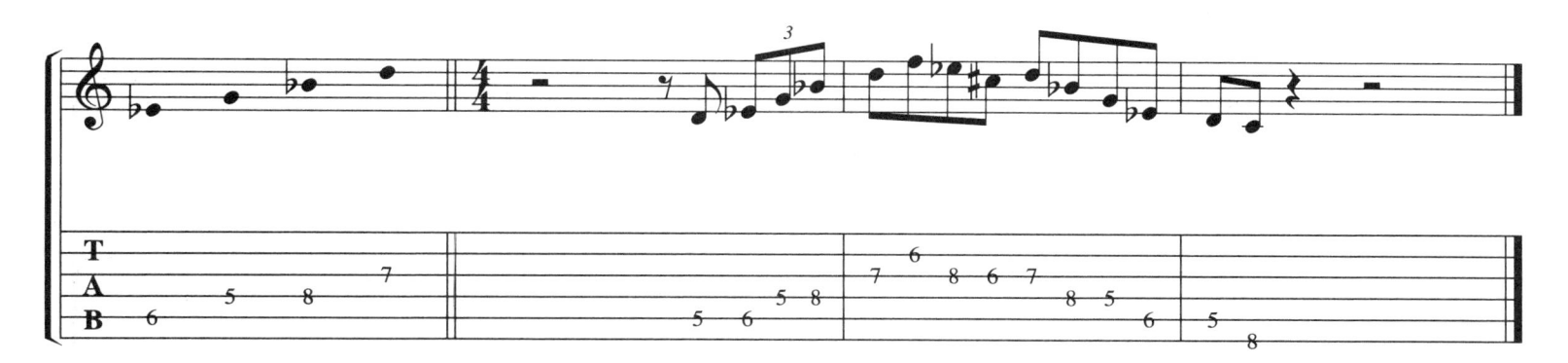

EXAMPLE 16 — MINOR 7♭5 ARPEGGIO ON 6

An Am7♭5 arpeggio will give you a Cm6 sound, which sounds darker than the E♭maj7 arpeggio.

SCOTT HENDERSON

EXAMPLE 17 — MINOR PENTATONIC SCALE ON 1, 2, AND 5

The C minor pentatonic over Cm7 is obvious. D and G minor pentatonic add a more Dorian sound. All three pentatonic scales contain notes from the B♭ major scale, which is C Dorian.

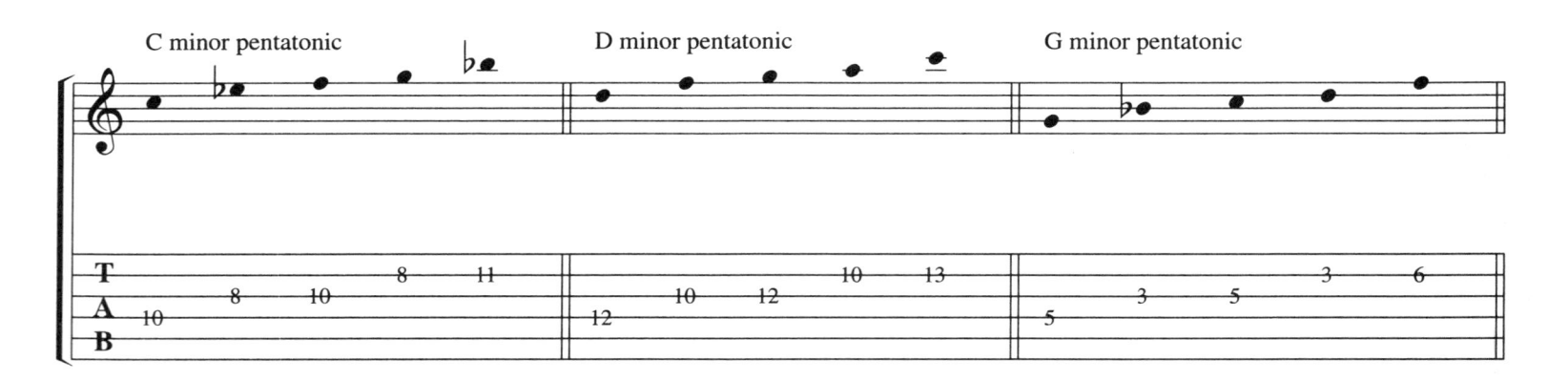

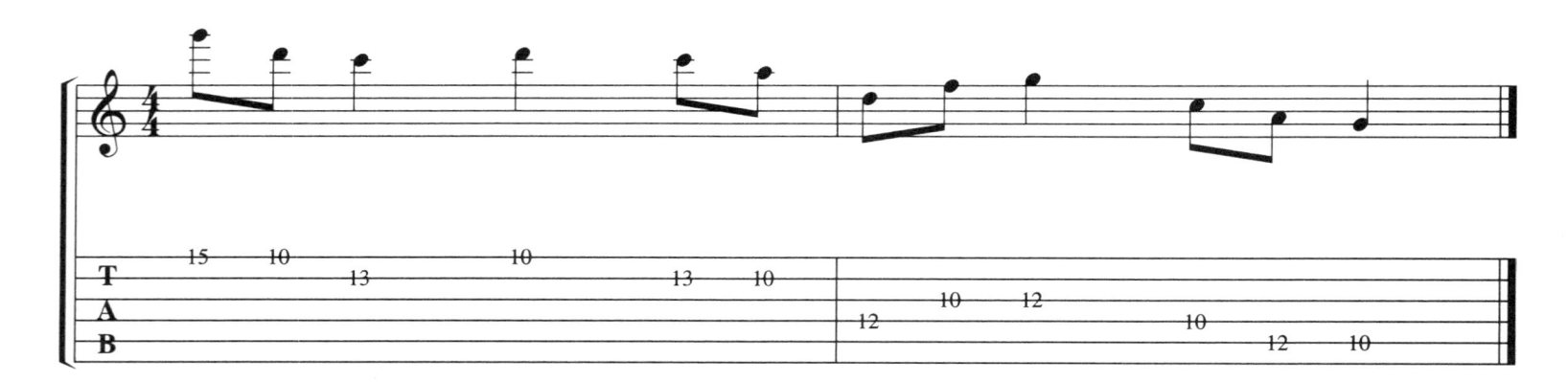

EXAMPLE 18 — MAJOR TRIADS ON ♭3, 4, AND ♭7

The notes in the E♭, F, and B♭ major triads can be found in the B♭ major scale (C Dorian). E♭ triad gives you a plain Cm7, while F and B♭ triads add a more Dorian sound.

SCOTT HENDERSON

The following ideas use the ♮7 instead of the ♭7 over Cm. One obvious reason to do this is if the chord has a major seventh in it [Cm(maj7)]. However, these ideas can also work over Cm7, because the major seventh will create some tension.

EXAMPLE 19 — MELODIC MINOR

This scale can be seen as a Dorian mode with a ♮7 instead of a ♭7.

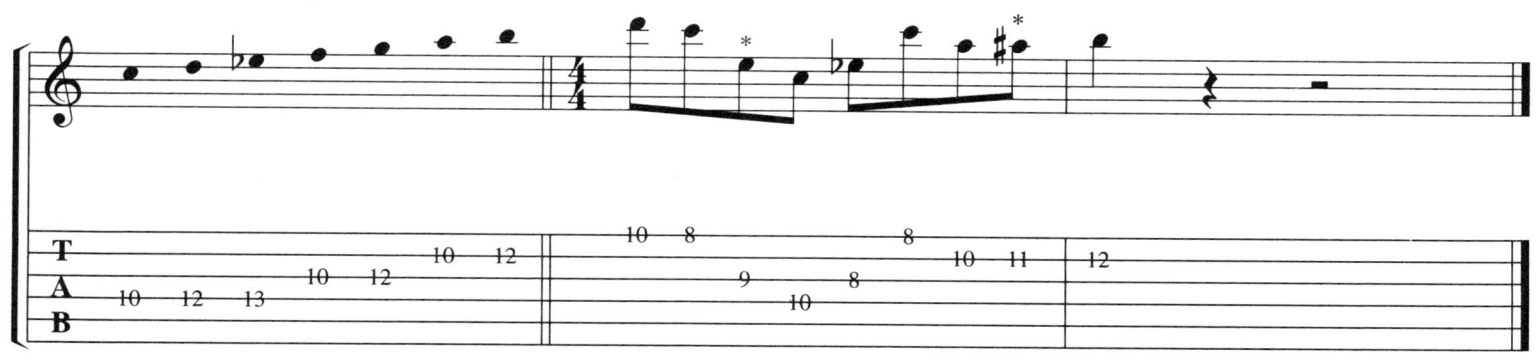

*Chromatic passing tones

EXAMPLE 20 — HARMONIC MINOR

An Aeolian mode with a ♮7 instead of a ♭7 produces the harmonic minor scale.

EXAMPLE 21 — MINOR WITH MAJOR 7 ARPEGGIO

Play the melodic minor scale without the 4th or 6th.

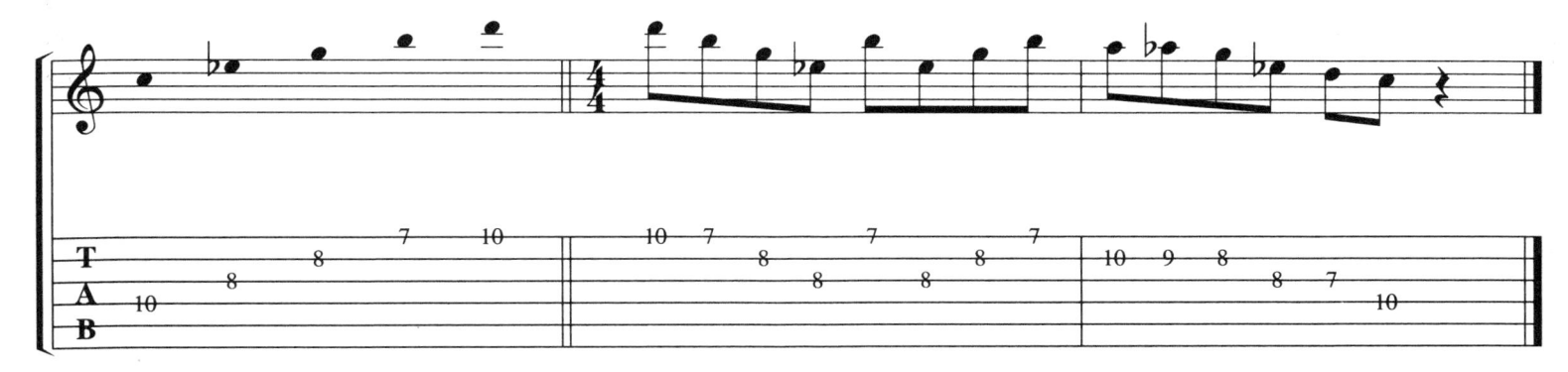

Scott Henderson

Example 22 — Major Triad on 5

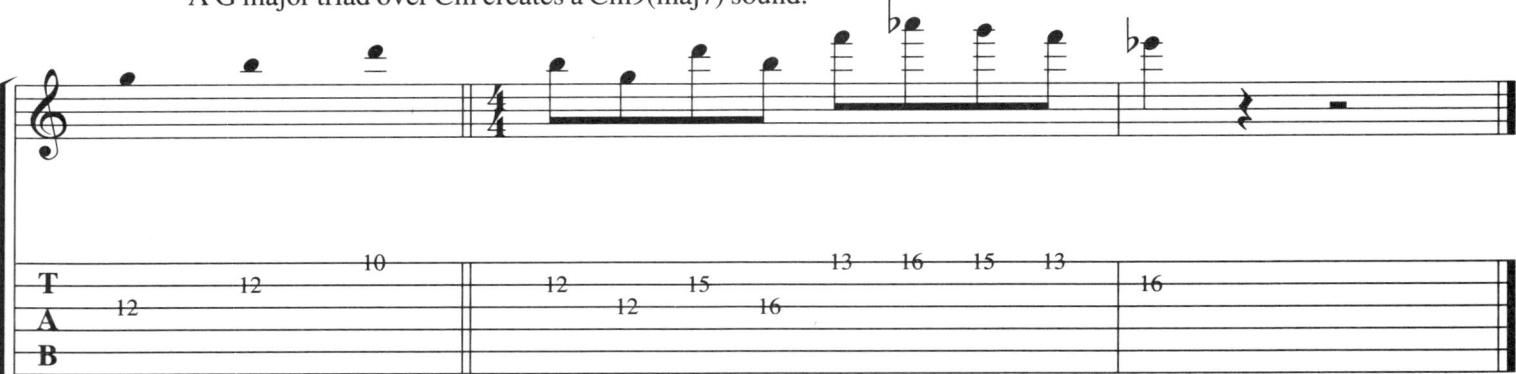

A G major triad over Cm creates a Cm9(maj7) sound.

The following ideas can be played over a Cm7♭5 chord.

Example 23 — C Minor 7♭5 Arpeggio

This is obviously the direct approach.

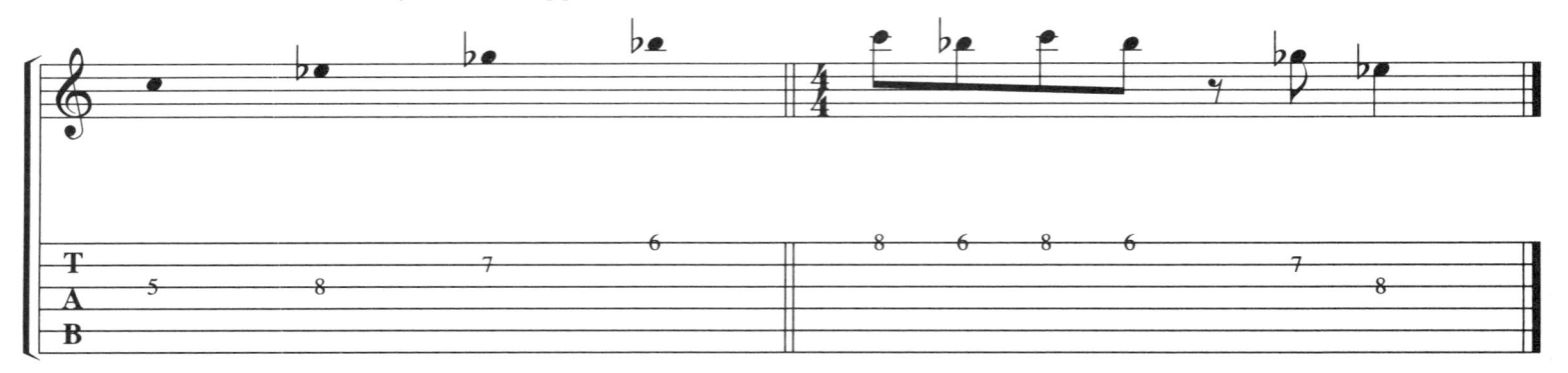

Example 24 — Locrian Mode

This is a major scale up a half step. Play a D♭ major scale over Cm7♭5.

This scale works, but it's not as hip as…

SCOTT HENDERSON

EXAMPLE 25 — SUPER LOCRIAN

As you probably guessed, it's a Locrian mode with a ♮2. Actually, it's a melodic minor scale starting on ♭3, and yes, it is another mode of the melodic minor scale. Play E♭ melodic minor over Cm7♭5.

*Chromatic passing tones

EXAMPLE 26 — MELODIC MINOR ARPEGGIO ON ♭3

Note that you can play the E♭m9(maj7) arpeggio any time you use the E♭ melodic minor scale. It's got a wider, more open sound.

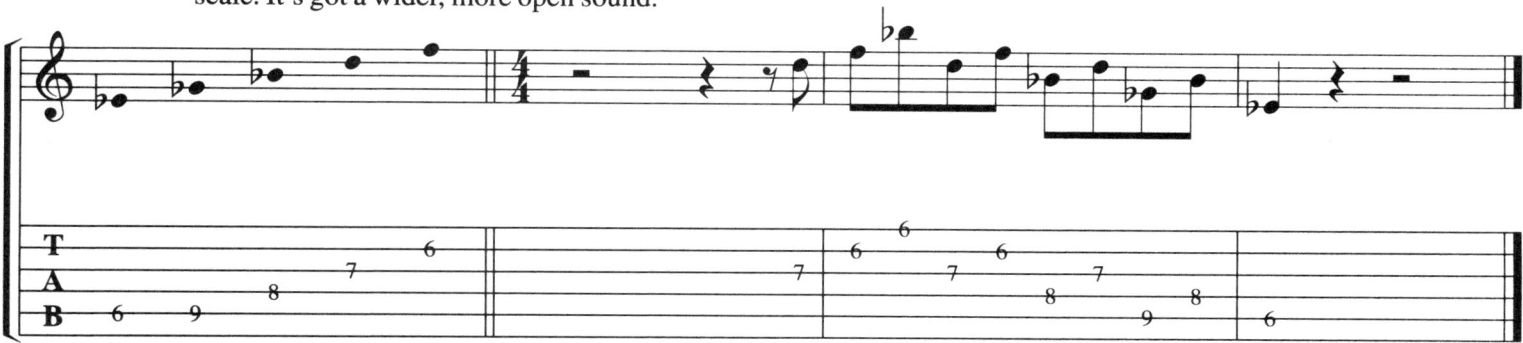

EXAMPLE 27 — MINOR PENTATONIC ON ♭3, 4, AND ♭7

These three scales, E♭, F, and B♭ minor pentatonic, contain notes from the D♭ major scale, which is C Locrian.

E♭ minor pentatonic   F minor pentatonic   B♭ minor pentatonic

SCOTT HENDERSON

All of the above Cm7♭5 ideas can also be used over Cm7 to take it a little "out." The Cm7♭5 arpeggio and the E♭ melodic minor scale/arpeggio aren't really that outside; they add the ♭5th, which is a bluesy note. The minor pentatonic scales and the Locrian mode take it farther out because they contain D♭ (the ♭9).

Another way to get outside over minor is by using the diminished scale. By playing a C diminished scale over Cm you get these "out" notes: ♭5th, ♯5th, and ♮7. Also, major triads on 2 and 7 sound cool over minor chords. Try D (Example 27a) and B (Example 27b) major triads over Cm; while you're at it, check out a B whole tone scale over Cm.

EXAMPLE 27A (NOT ON CD)

*Chromatic passing tone

EXAMPLE 27B (NOT ON CD)

The following ideas can be played over a C suspended chord.

EXAMPLE 28 — MAJOR 7 ARPEGGIO ON ♭7

The B♭maj7 arpeggio creates the sound of C13sus4.

SCOTT HENDERSON

EXAMPLE 29 — MAJOR TRIADS ON ♭7 AND 4

B♭ and F triads create a true C suspended sound — no thirds.

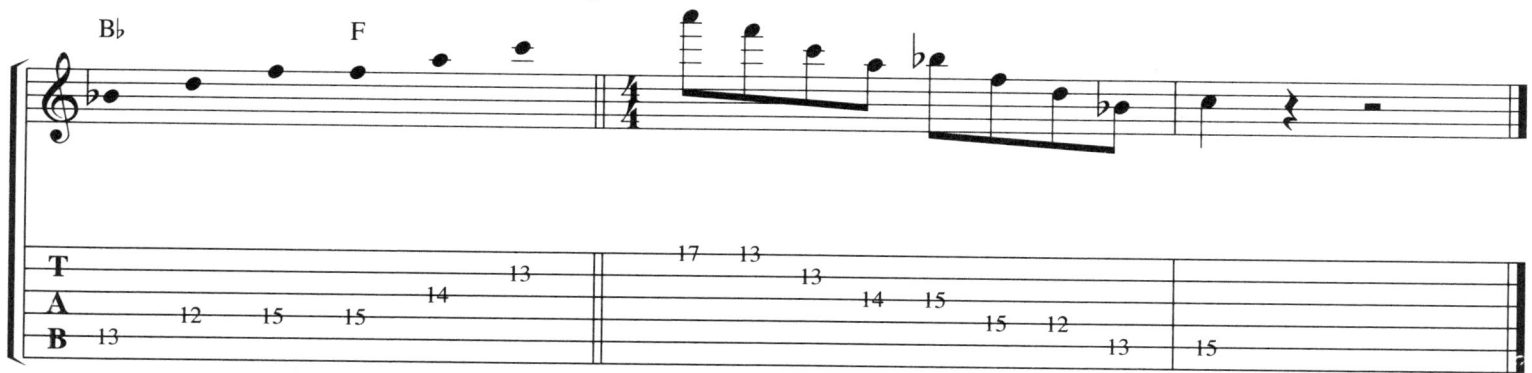

EXAMPLE 30 — MINOR PENTATONIC ON 2 AND 5

D and G minor pentatonic scales also create a true C suspended sound — no thirds.

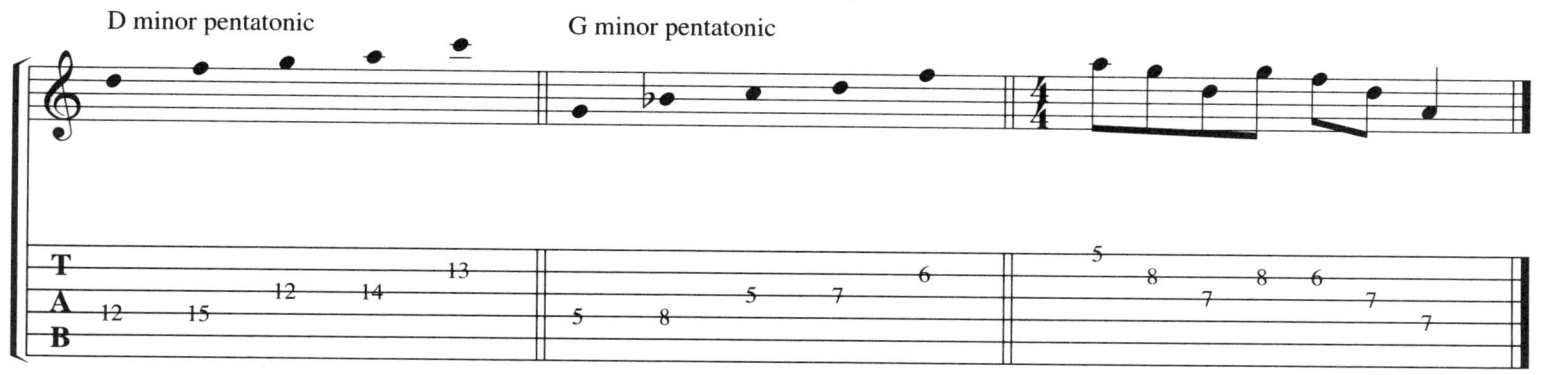

The following ideas can be played over C Phrygian chords: Csus4(♭9) or B♭m/C.

EXAMPLE 31 — PHRYGIAN MODE

This is a major scale starting on the ♭6. For Csus4(♭9), play A♭ major scale.

SCOTT HENDERSON

EXAMPLE 32 — MELODIC MINOR ON ♭7

This is another mode of the melodic minor scale. For Csus4(♭9), play the B♭ melodic minor scale. The result is Phrygian mode with a ♮6(A) instead of a ♭6(A♭).

EXAMPLE 33 — MINOR (MAJOR 7) ARPEGGIO ON ♭7

Play the B♭m(maj7) arpeggio over Csus4(♭9).

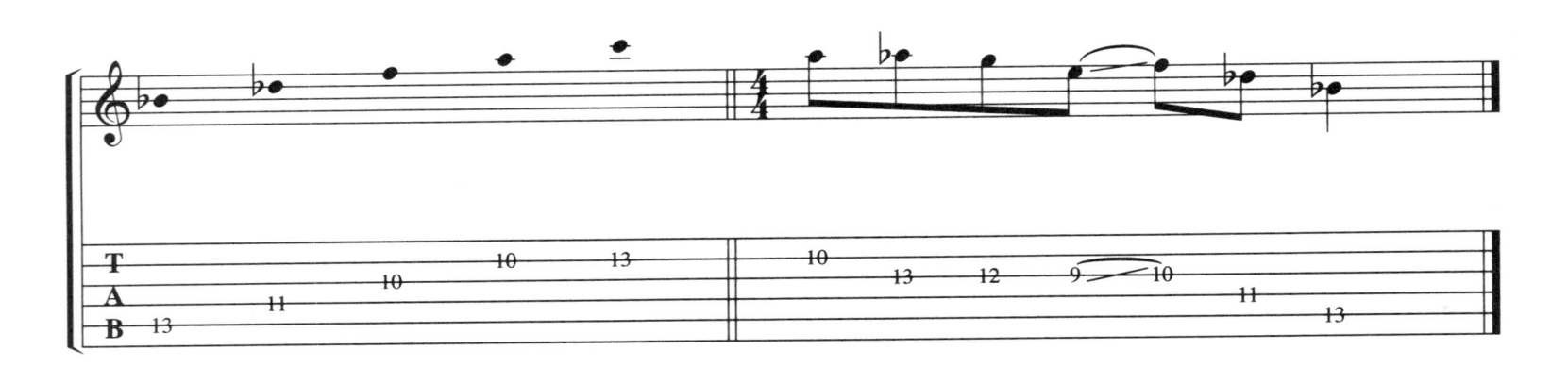

EXAMPLE 34 — MINOR 7♭5 ARPEGGIO ON 5

A Gm7♭5 arpeggio played over Csus4(♭9) outlines the chord really well.

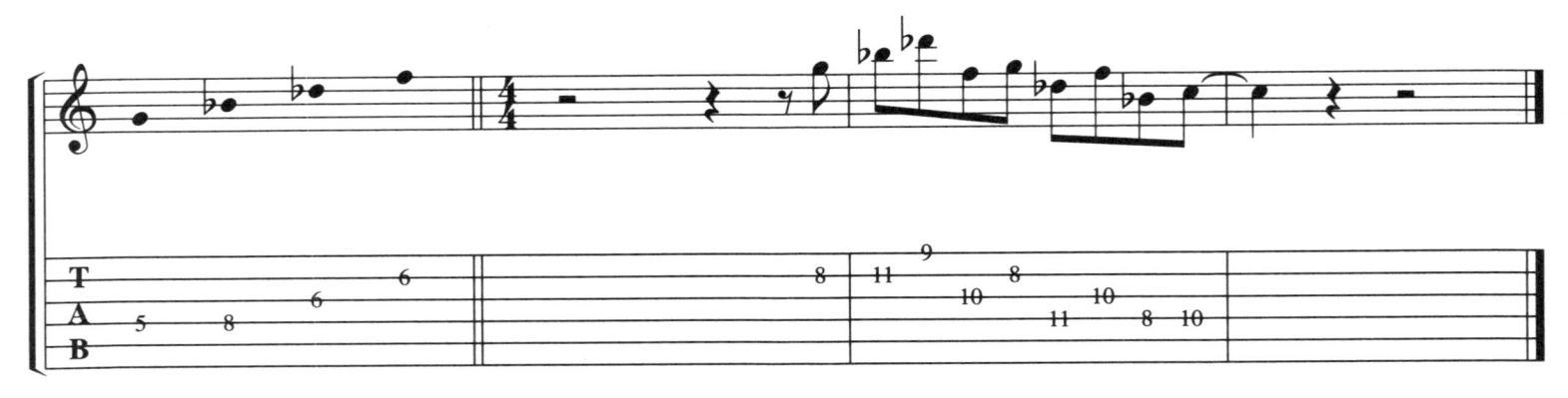

SCOTT HENDERSON

The following ideas can be played over a C7 chord.

EXAMPLE 35 — MIXOLYDIAN MODE

This is a major scale starting on the fourth degree. For C7, play an F major scale. You can add E♭ to this scale to make it sound bluesier.

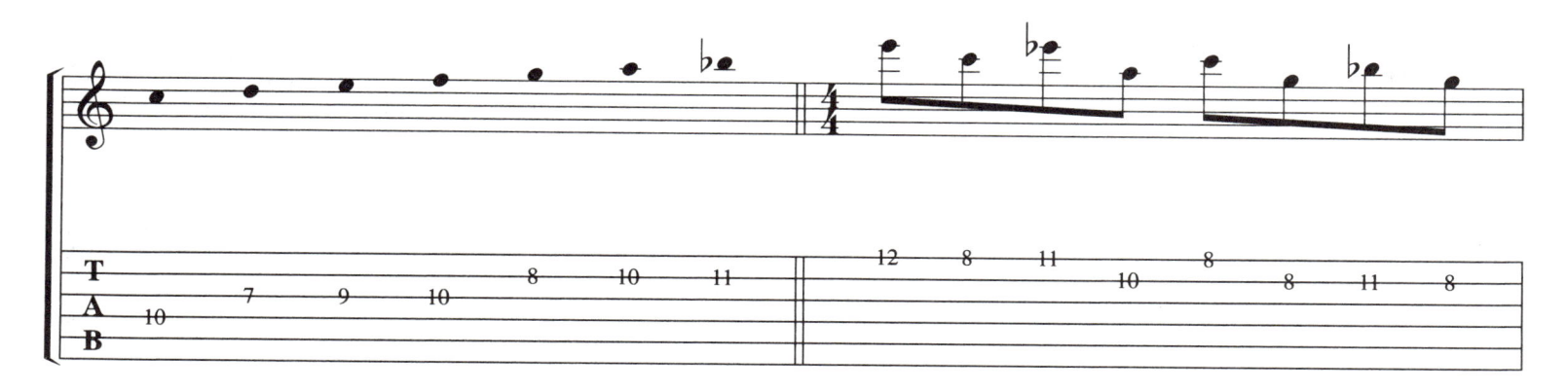

EXAMPLE 36 — MINOR 7♭5 ARPEGGIO ON 3

An Em7♭5 arpeggio played over C7 will give you a C9 sound.

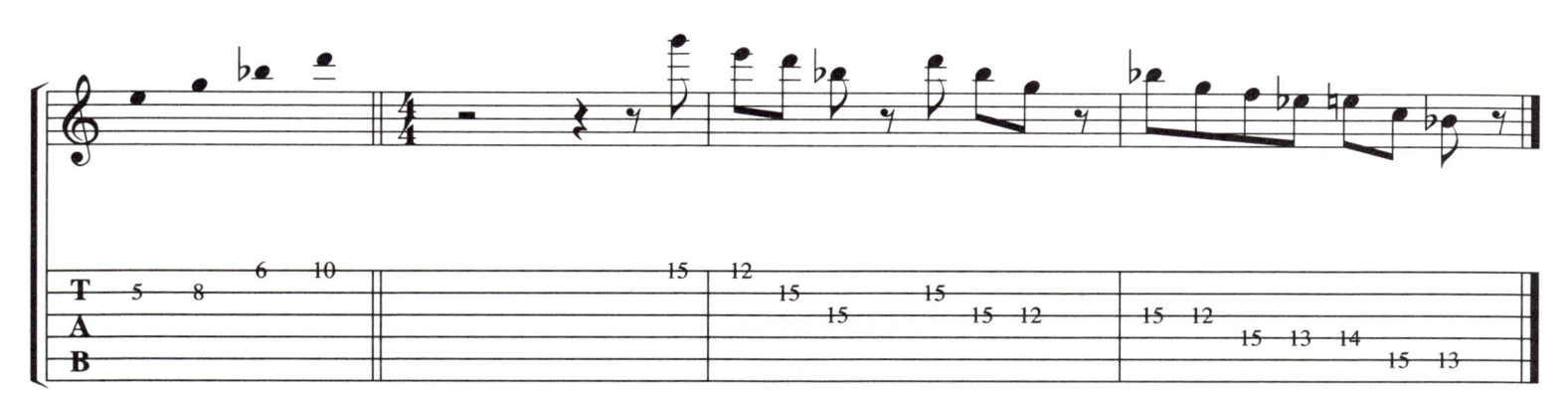

→ = C mixolydian

SCOTT HENDERSON

EXAMPLE 37 — MINOR PENTATONIC ON 1, 2, 5, AND 6

Experiment with those blues licks again! The D and G minor pentatonic scales have the passing F (which is an "avoid" note), so C and A minor pentatonic are the best choices. All of the notes that lie across the 3rd, 5th, 8th, 10th, 15th, 20th, and 22nd frets contain notes from these four scales. Experiment by stretching out and playing the notes on those frets over C7.

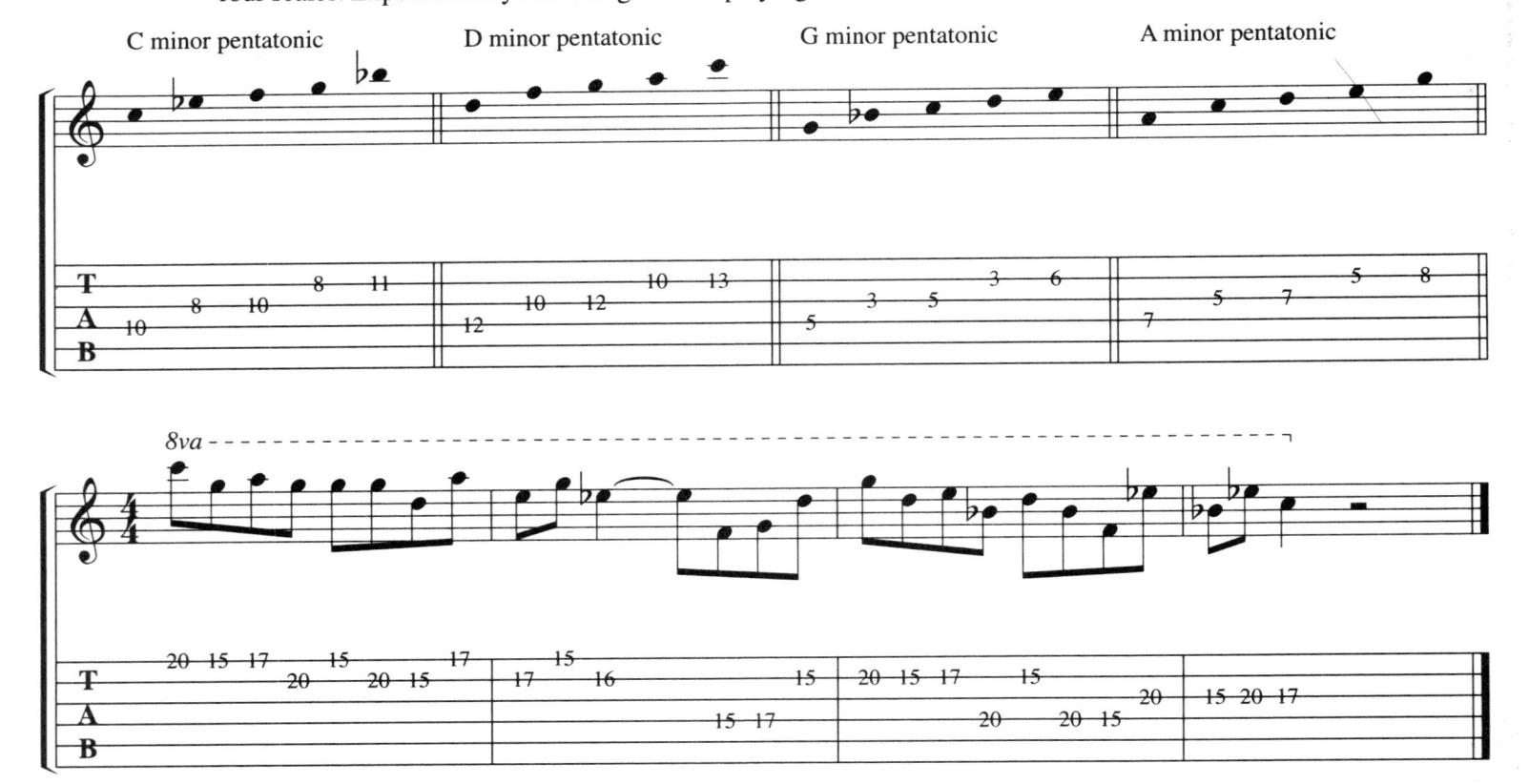

The following ideas will add the #11 to the C7 chord, which is a common extension.

EXAMPLE 38 — LYDIAN DOMINANT SCALE

This is the Lydian mode with a ♭7. Actually, it's just a melodic minor scale starting on the fifth degree. For C7, play a G melodic minor scale — yes, it's another mode of melodic minor.

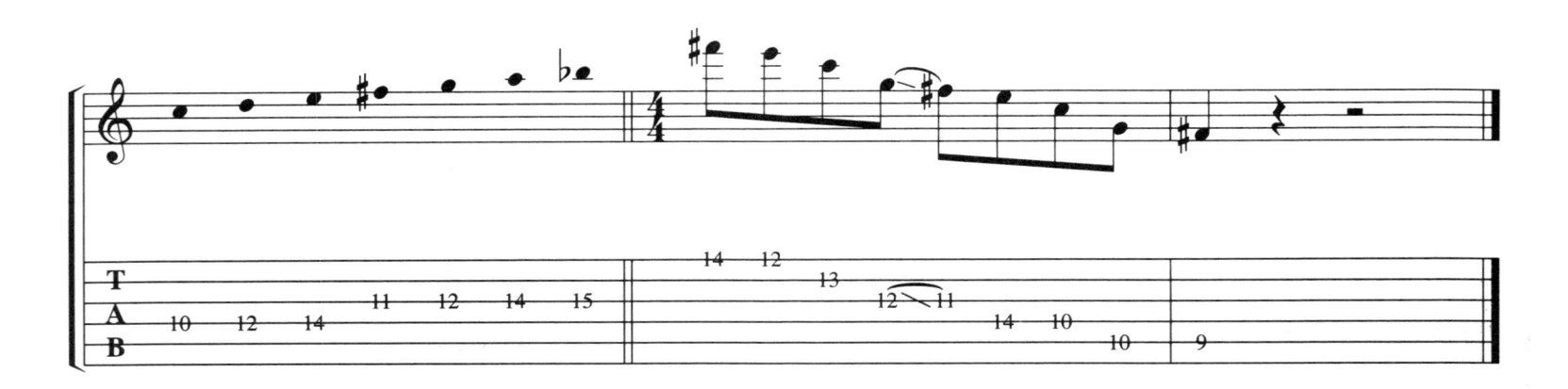

▶ 60

EXAMPLE 39 — MINOR (MAJOR 9) ON 5

The Gm(maj9) arpeggio creates the 13#11 sound when played over C7.

EXAMPLE 40 — MAJOR TRIAD ON 2

The D triad over C7 covers the upper extensions of the C13#11 chord.

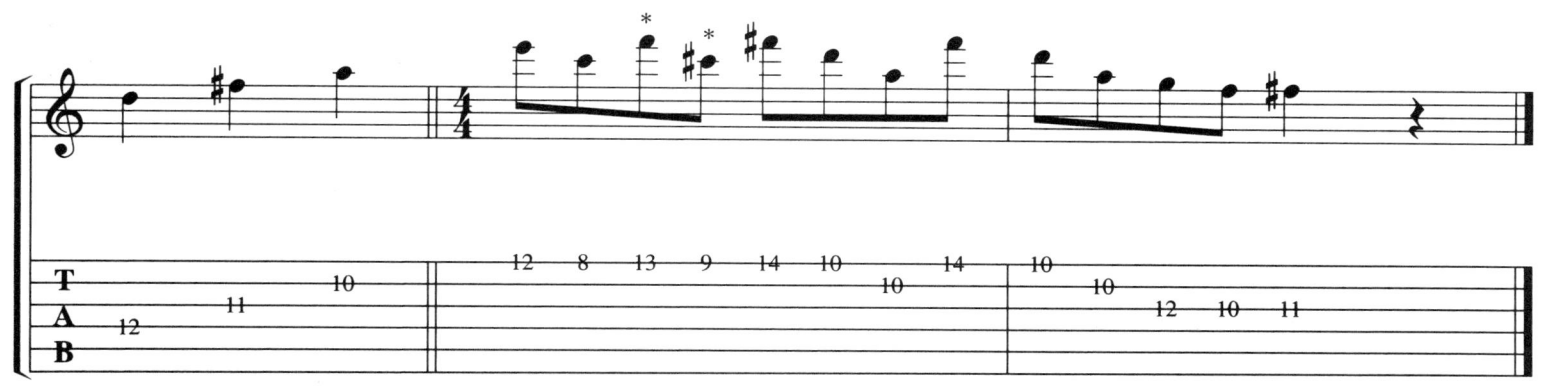

*Chromatic passing tones

EXAMPLE 41 — MINOR 7♭5 ARPEGGIO ON ♭5

Play G♭m7♭5 over C13#11 and see how it works for you. This is not one of my favorites, but here it is anyway.

Scott Henderson

The following ideas can be played over C altered dominant (C7alt) chords; the best chords for each application are indicated.

Example 42 — Half-Step Diminished

This is a diminished scale starting with a half-step. It works best over C7#9b9 and C13#9b9.

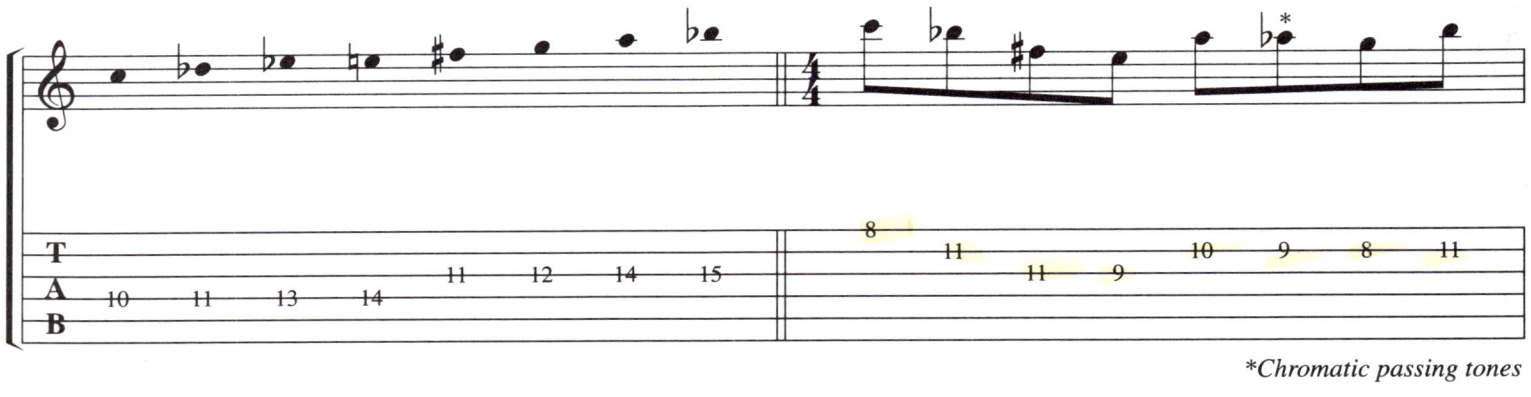

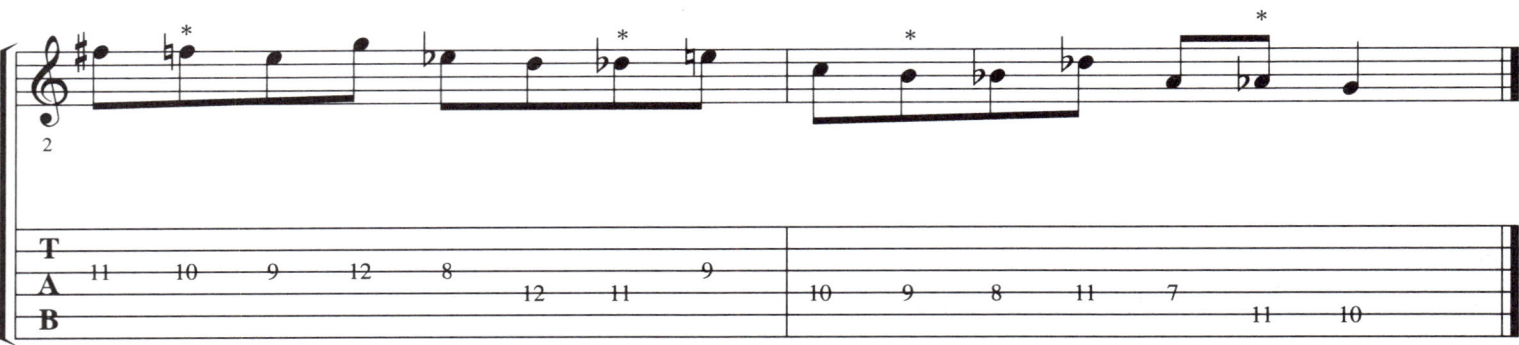

*Chromatic passing tones

Example 43 — Altered Scale

Here is another mode of the melodic minor scale. Over altered dominant chords, play the melodic minor scale up a half-step. For C7alt, play Db melodic minor. This works best over C7#5 and C7#5b9#9.

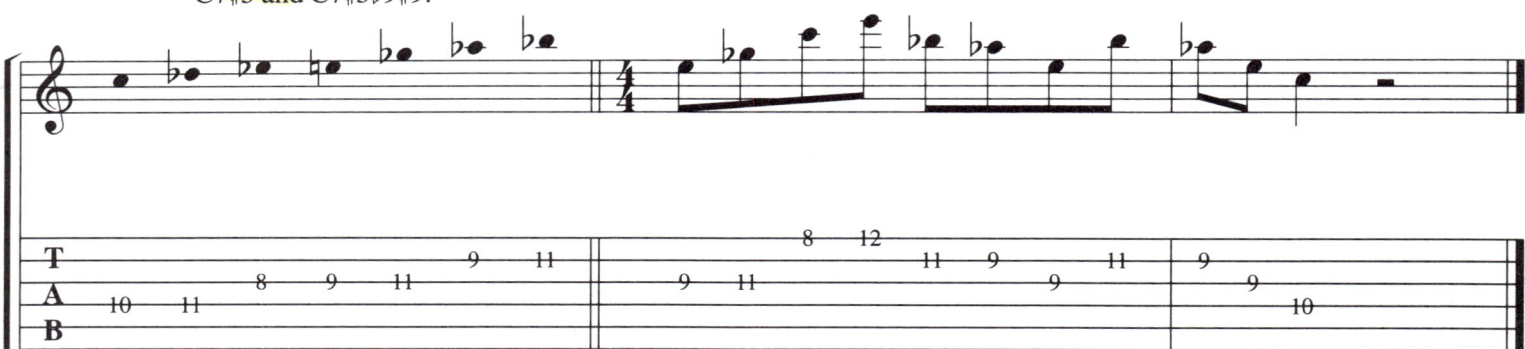

Example 44 — Minor (Major 7) Arpeggio up a Half-Step

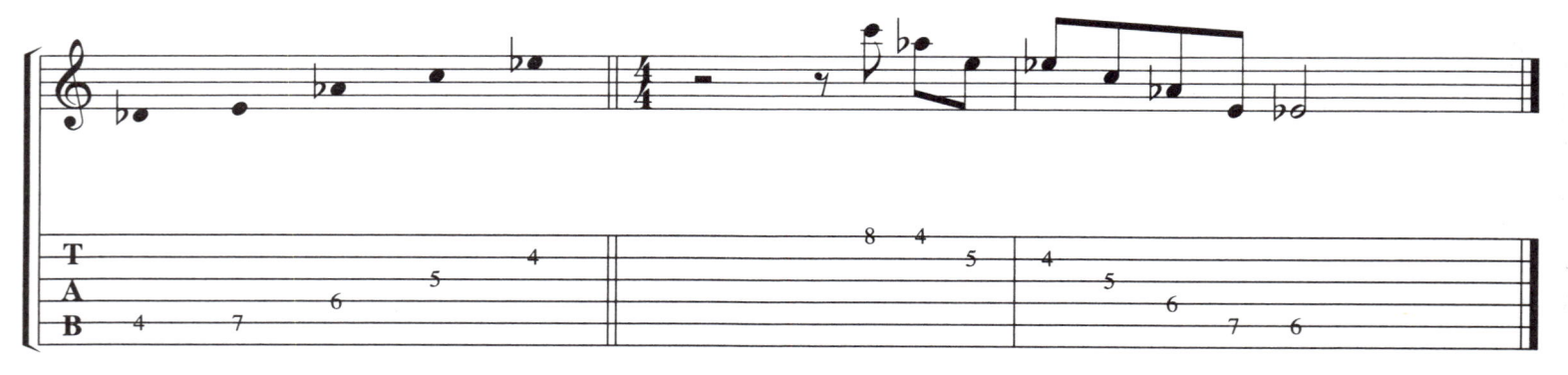

SCOTT HENDERSON

EXAMPLE 45 — MELODIC MINOR ON ♭7

The same B♭ melodic minor scale we used over the Phrygian chords will work for C13♭9♯9.

*Chromatic passing tones

EXAMPLE 46 — MINOR (MAJOR 7) ARPEGGIO ON ♭7

B♭m(maj7) works great over C13♭9.

EXAMPLE 47 — MINOR 7♭5 ARPEGGIO ON ♭7

A B♭m7♭5 arpeggio played over C7alt outlines the C7♯5♭9 chord.

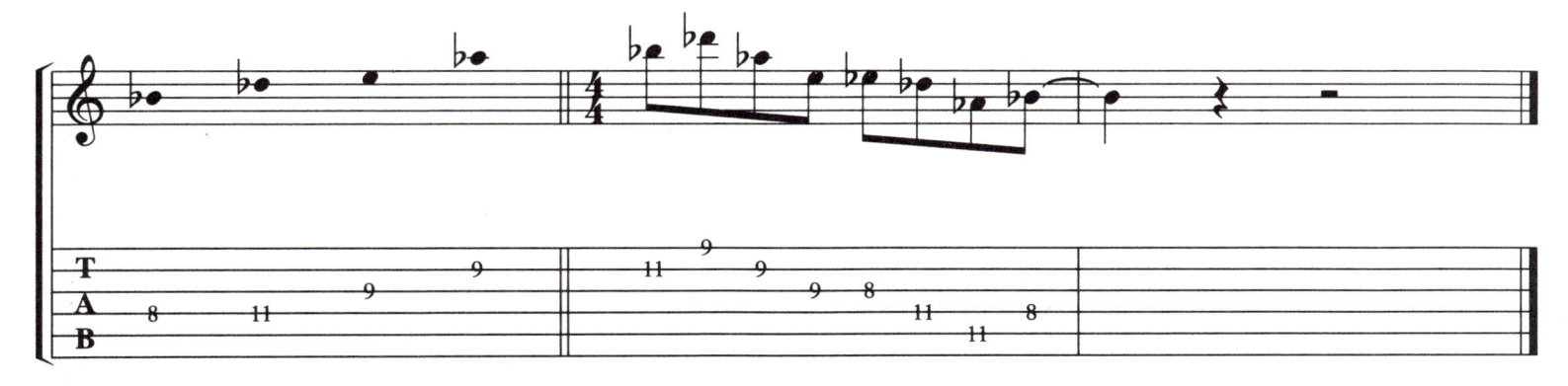

63

SCOTT HENDERSON

EXAMPLE 48 — MINOR PENTATONIC ON 1, ♭3, 4, AND ♭7

The notes in the C, E♭, F, and B♭ minor pentatonic scales sound great over C7♯5.

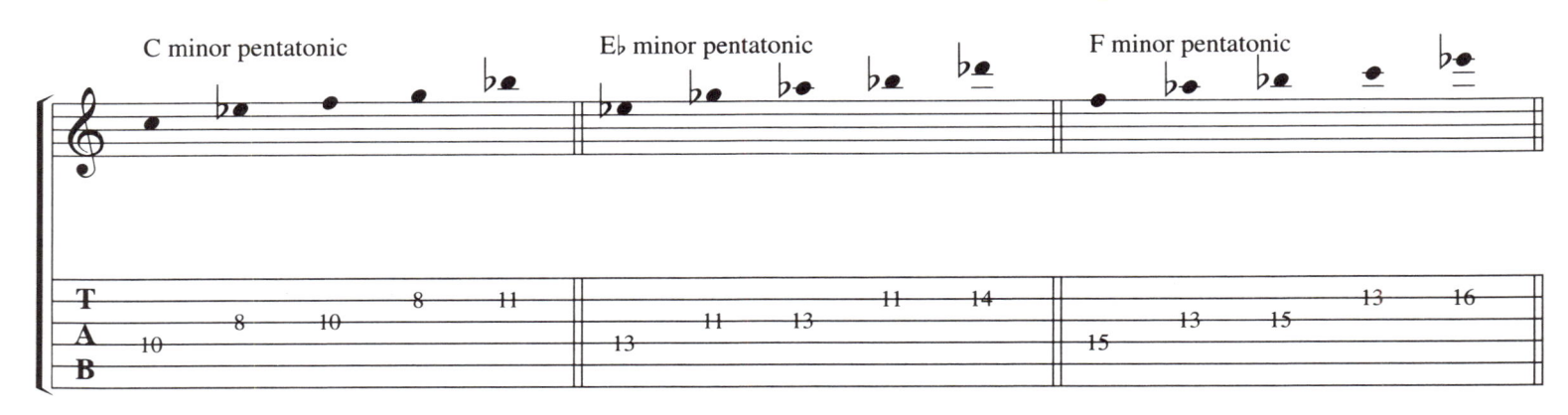

EXAMPLE 49 — MAJOR TRIADS ON 1, ♭3, ♭5, AND 6

The notes in the C, E♭, G♭, and A major triads contain notes from the C (half-step first) diminished scale.

SCOTT HENDERSON

EXAMPLE 50 — HARMONIC MINOR ON 4

An F harmonic minor scale played over C7 gives you the sound of C7#5b9.

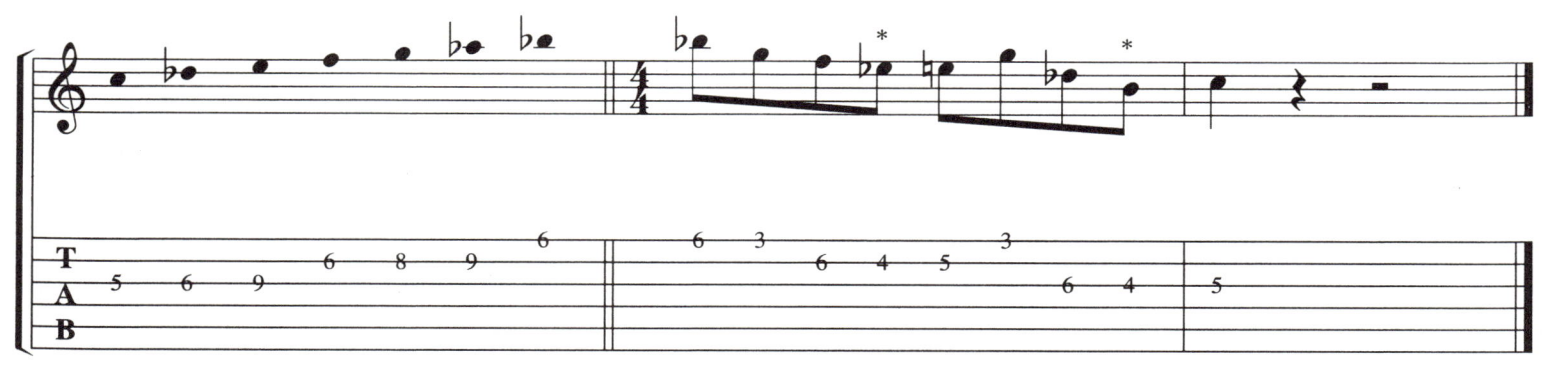

*Chromatic passing tones

EXAMPLE 51 — WHOLE TONE SCALE

Since there is a D natural in the C whole tone scale, it doesn't sound good over C7 chords with a b9 or #9. It sounds best over C9#5.

EXAMPLE 52 — DIMINISHED ARPEGGIO

You can play a diminished arpeggio off the 3rd, 5th, b7th, or b9th of an altered dominant chord. It gives you the 7b9 sound.

SCOTT HENDERSON

The following can be played over C diminished:

EXAMPLE 53 — C DIMINISHED SCALE, WHOLE STEP FIRST

EXAMPLE 54 — MAJOR TRIADS ON 4, 7, 9, AND ♭6

For a C diminished chord, try F, B, D, and A♭ triad arpeggios.

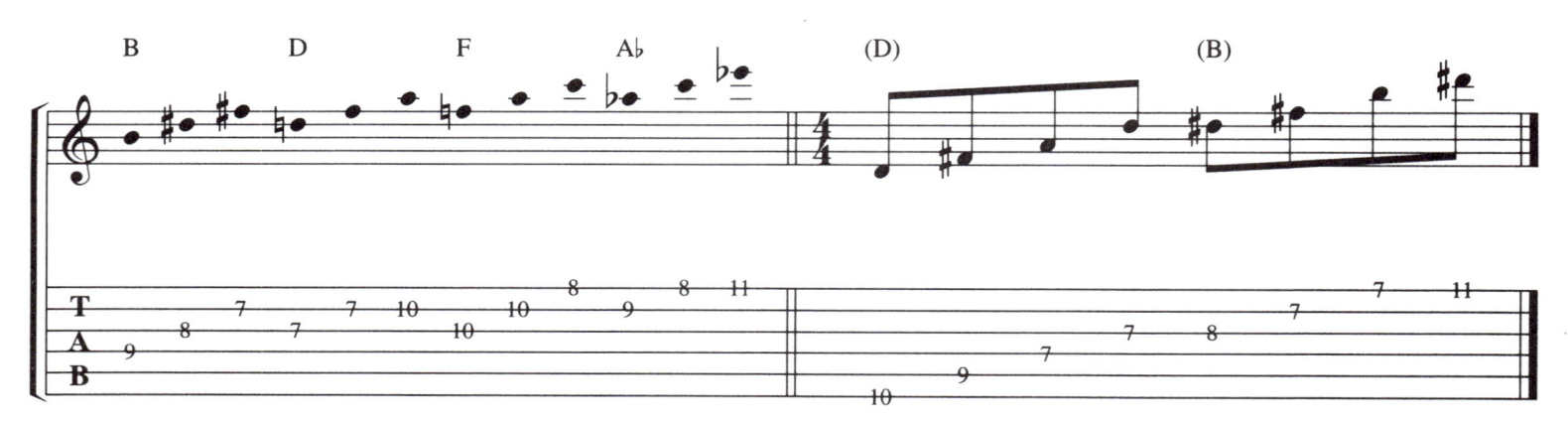

Remember: All the example lines are interchangeable. For example, the A melodic minor lick (Example 10) could be played over A♭7 altered, D7#11, B Phrygian etc.

Finally, my suggestion for this lesson is: take it slow! Work on one concept at a time. Instead of just playing the scales or arpeggios up and down, try to create melodies with them and incorporate rhythmic ideas — in other words, make them song-like. Everything you study should be put into the context of a tune, so you can develop your phrasing and musicality as well. Often when players try to expand their vocabulary, it comes at the expense of their phrasing. So try to practice these ideas in a musical way. Make a practice tape and play, and most important of all — have fun!

STEVE LUKATHER

STEVE LUKATHER WAS BORN AND RAISED IN LOS ANGELES AND began playing the guitar at age seven. Inspired like many musicians his age by the Beatles and other British Invasion bands, he joined groups while still very young. In high school, one of Steve's bands also included guitarist Mike Landau, Steve Porcaro on keyboards, Carlos Vega on drums, and bassist John Pierce. "I used to hang out with older guys who could play better than me," Lukather recalls, "sponge off one, and once I'd learned that, I'd go on to the next."

He began studying with noted jazz guitarist Jimmy Wyble (Red Norvo, Benny Goodman) at age 16. Until then, he had been self-taught and was already proficient at rock 'n' roll. Wyble expanded Steve's knowledge of positions, scales, notes and relationships, and opened his ears to many different types of music.

Steve's first record date was with with pianist Jai Winding. Also playing the session were Michael and Jeff Porcaro, Steve's high school buddies who, along with keyboardist David Paich, were about to go on the road with Boz Scaggs's *Silk Degrees* tour. Soon afterwards, Scaggs's guitarist quit, and opportunity came knocking for Steve Lukather: the 19-year-old was tapped for the guitar slot and joined the tour. It was Steve's first experience with big-time rock — but it would not be his last.

As word spread about the new young guitarist, Steve's career took off. Soon he was playing twenty sessions a week with recording artists such as Alice Cooper *(From The Inside)*, Boz Scaggs *(Down Two Then Left)*, Hall and Oates *(Along The Red Ledge)*, and Earth, Wind, and Fire *(I Am)*.

In 1978 Lukather, with longtime cohorts Jeff and Steve Porcaro and David Paich, formed the rock group Toto. Their first album, *Toto,* hit the top of the pop charts with the single "Hold The Line," featuring a searing Lukather guitar solo. The band followed up with *Hydra, Turn Back, Toto IV, Isolation, Fahrenheit, The Seventh One, Past To Present,* and their current release, *Kingdom of Desire.* The massively successful *Toto IV* won five Grammy awards in 1983 and yielded two of that year's top-selling singles, "Rosanna" and "Africa."

In addition to his work with Toto, Steve maintains a busy studio schedule. He has recently appeared on recordings by Paul McCartney *(Give My Regards To Broad Street)*, Eric Clapton *(Behind the Sun)*, Michael Jackson *(Thriller)*, and Don Henley *(Dirty Laundry)*. His solo albums include *Lukather* and the soon-to-be-released *Candy Man.* Steve has also written songs for Richard Marx, Chicago, Alice Cooper, George Benson, Sheena Easton, Kenny Rogers, Donna Summers and Boz Scaggs. George Benson's recording of Steve's "Turn Your Love Around" gave Steve his fourth Grammy Award for R&B Record of the Year in 1983.

In his chapter, Steve discusses ways to use sophisticated harmonic and rhythmic concepts to intensify rock and pop solos.

STEVE LUKATHER

LESSON 1 ▶ EXPANDING YOUR BLUES VOCABULARY

At one point I really wanted to be a bebop guitar player, but I realized it was futile; I couldn't dedicate my life to this style. I like well-played, well-crafted commercial music, but I also like to sneak some musicality into it. So I decided to use jazz to enhance my rock playing. I play straight-ahead rock with some jazz concepts mixed in, as opposed to jazz with a rock sound.

When I was in high school, I heard Larry Carlton on the Steely Dan album "The Royal Scam," playing jazz-type lines with a distorted rock tone. That was really a turning point for me. I'd been searching for my own voice and Larry's playing helped me get an idea of what I wanted to sound like. But to do what he was doing, I needed to expand my musical vocabulary in a big way. That's when I started working through scales, modes and arpeggios.

I needed to come up with musical lines using this information, so I developed a practice method to put the knowledge to practical use. I would play chord changes into a tape recorder, then play over the changes until my lines made sense. My goal was to develop my ear and my melodic sense. I started out with simple, one-key changes and gradually increased the level of difficulty. The examples below use fairly easy changes. Record them and experiment. Example 1 sounds like A minor pentatonic to most players, but there's no reason not to use A Mixolydian or A Lydian dominant. You can use more sophisticated scales and still retain the flavor of the tune!

EXAMPLE 1

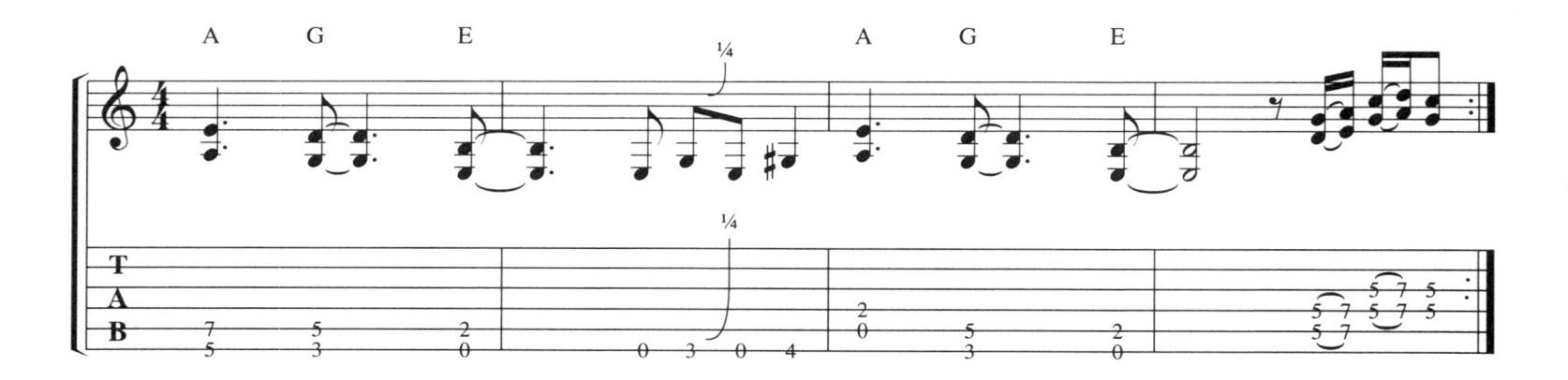

In Example 2, you could use D minor pentatonic, but you would probably play more interesting lines off the chord tones. Check out the patterns in Example 2a — they're all in fifth or sixth position, so they're within easy reach.

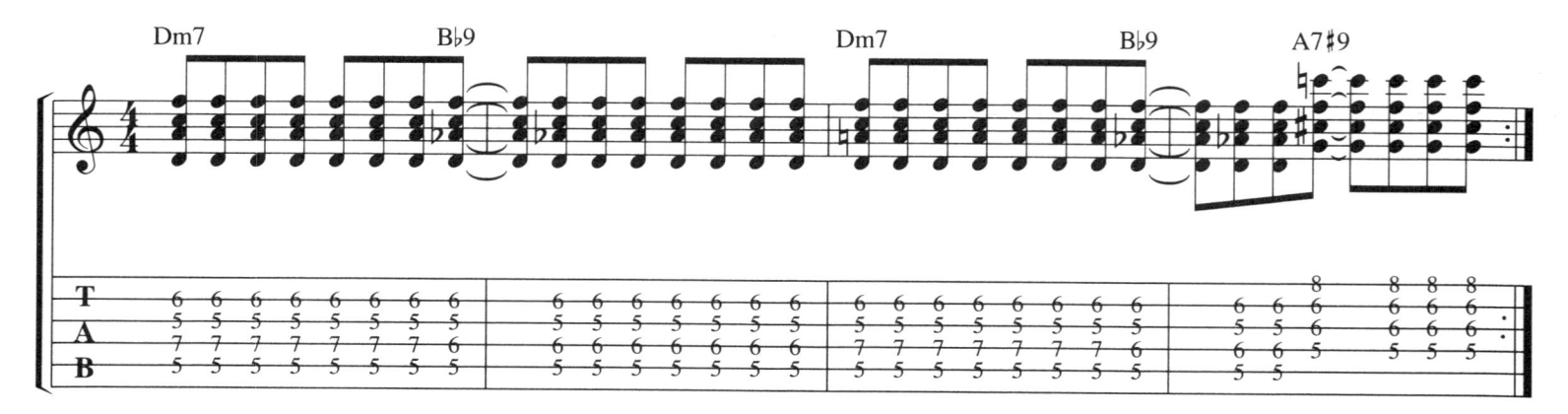

EXAMPLE 2

STEVE LUKATHER

EXAMPLE 2A

In Example 3, the E Mixolydian scale is used to add a funky sound to a stock progression. Try the lick in Example 3a.

EXAMPLE 3

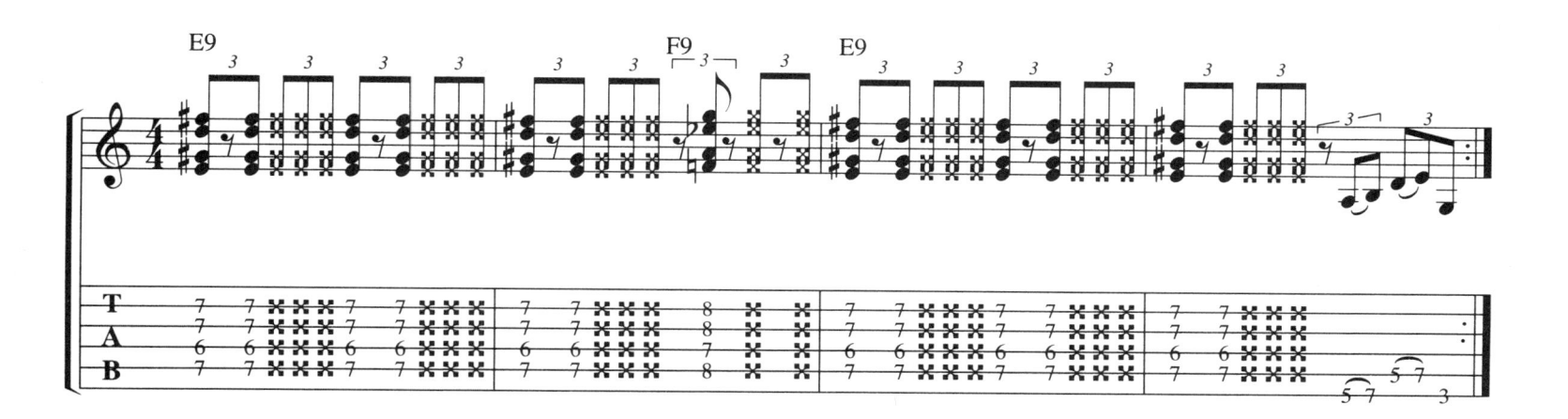

EXAMPLE 3A

STEVE LUKATHER

Basic blues is another good progression to use in practicing your new sounds. In Example 4, we'll be playing blues in the key of A. Everybody has Lick 1 below in their repertoire. The other licks are examples of how I play the blues. I like to use 3rds, 7ths, and 9ths, in addition to the stock pentatonic licks. Lick 2 centers around the 7th and 11th of the chord and Lick 3 uses 4ths. Lick 4 is a "country-style" lick; if you're playing with a rock band and you sneak some of this in, people are going to notice.

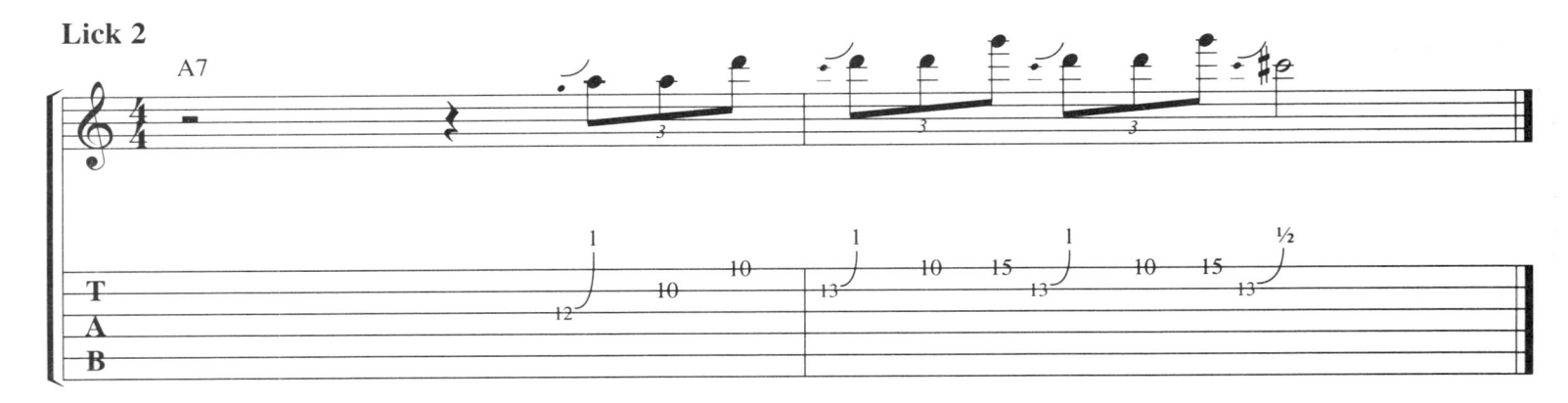

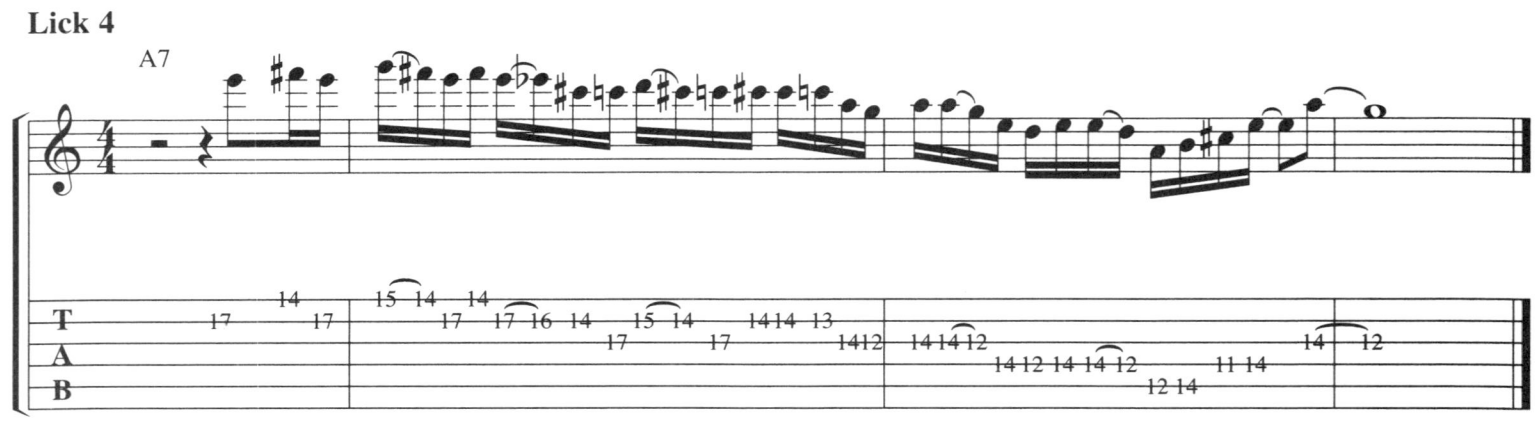

EXAMPLE 4

STEVE LUKATHER

A lot of people are afraid to "commit" (i.e., change scale or arpeggio) when they go to the IV chord. The licks below outline the D7 chord. Making *each* chord change increases your melodic quality. Check out Example 5.

EXAMPLE 5

You can make yourself sound really impressive over the most basic rock and jazz progressions. Everything else is just a permutation of the blues anyway. You can add more notes to each chord through extensions (adding the 9th or 11th to a dominant 7 chord), or by adding extra chords to the basic progression (as in jazz or bebop style blues). Many of my ideas come from these two concepts. By expanding my note choices, I can create more interesting lines. In Example 6, a basic 12-bar blues form is played using a jazz-style progression. If you think about the more complex changes and chord structure when you solo, even over a basic progression, your lines will be more interesting.

EXAMPLE 6

STEVE LUKATHER

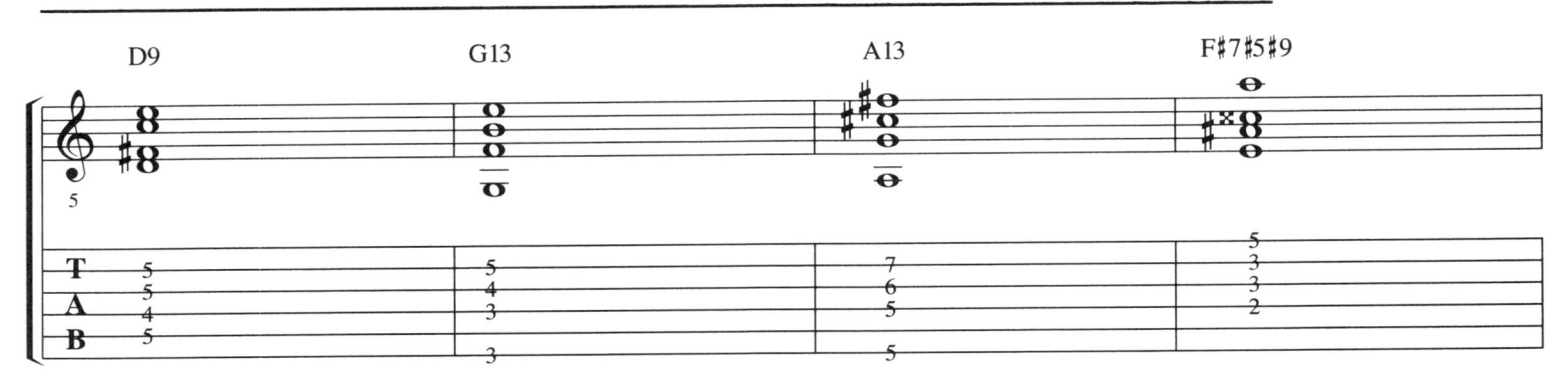

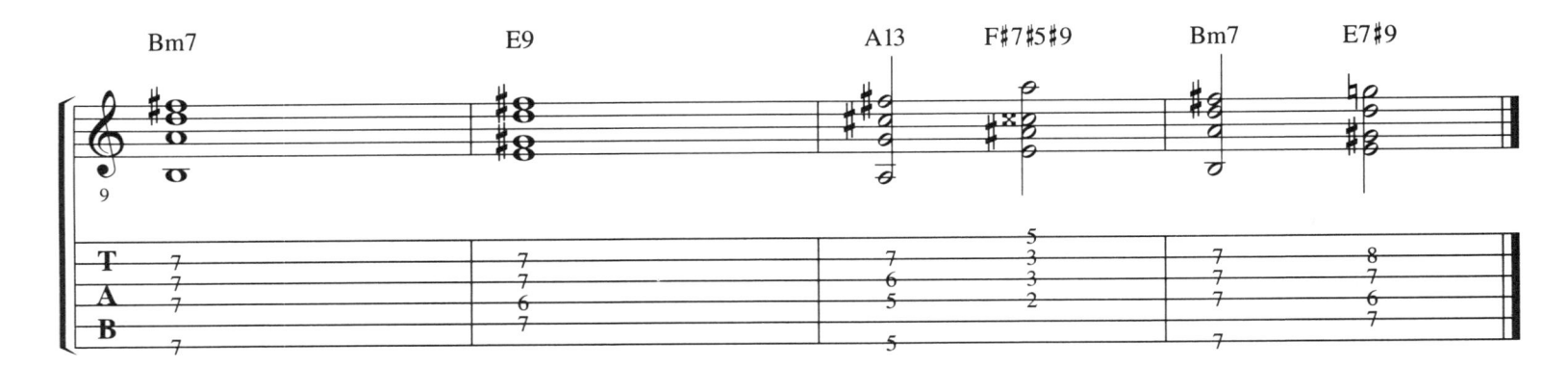

Instead of using scales exclusively, you can apply chord shapes to your lines. This will help you find all the important notes and sweeter notes more easily. Working with chord tones allows you to get out of that "block" or pattern that guitarists often play from. Example 7 gives ideas to play over A7 that includes the 7th, 9th, 11th, and 13th. You'll notice that I like to "double-time" my figures.

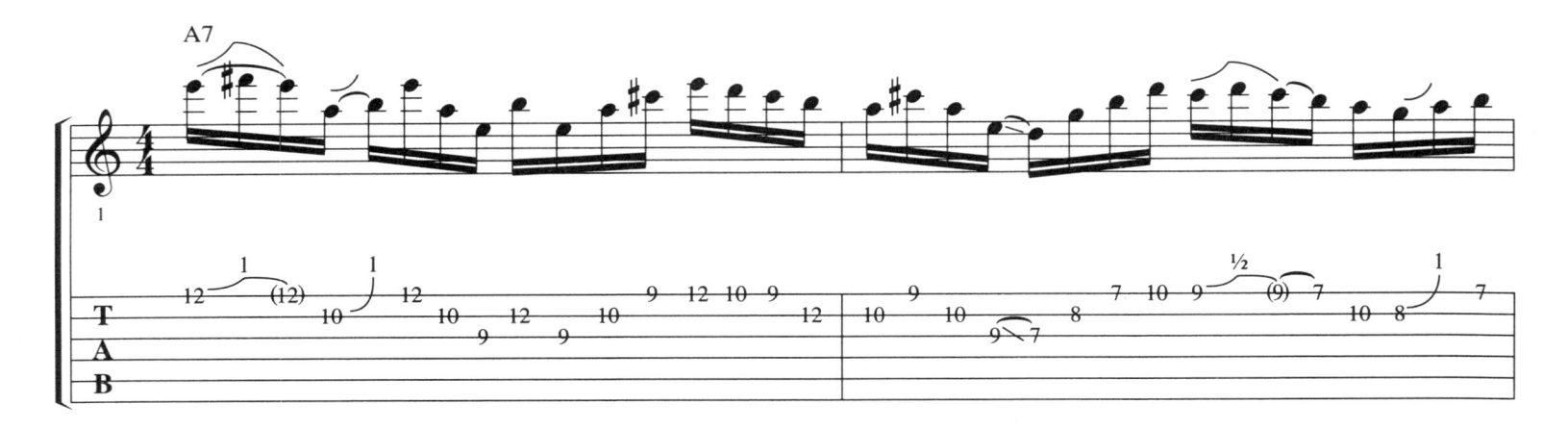

EXAMPLE 7

STEVE LUKATHER

To make this work, you need enough facility on the instrument to move from one idea to the next without thinking about it. And to achieve such facility, you have to practice — alone, by trial and error or playing with another guitarist. If you play with another guitarist, try to avoid preconceived ideas. Guitarists seem, more than other musicians, to fall into patterns. The idea is to get away from all those patterns and rediscover the guitar. Go back and forth, with each player taking sixteen choruses. That's what jamming is all about. It's ear training — trying to play what you hear. On the gig you're being judged; but when you jam, it's safe to make mistakes.

LESSON 2 ▶ RHYTHM GUITAR: A LOST ART

It seems like people have almost forgotten about rhythm guitar. A lot of players have amazing chops but can't play rhythm; often they can't lock in with a drummer. I'm lucky to have played with quite a few great rhythm guitar players, like David T. Walker, Wah Wah Watson, Lee Ritenour, Paul Jackson Jr., Ray Parker and Jay Graydon. I learned a lot from those people; I was exposed to many different styles and it got me thinking more seriously about the place of rhythm guitar. For example, you might be playing with drums, bass, congas, keyboards and a guy soloing, and you need to find a part that fits — a riff that becomes part of the groove. With an awareness of good rhythm guitar playing, and a little trial and error, you'll find a figure that works. Again, jamming with other players allows you to experiment (and make mistakes) because you're in a safe environment.

Example 8 is a common chord progression. We'll use this as the foundation and create the other parts from here.

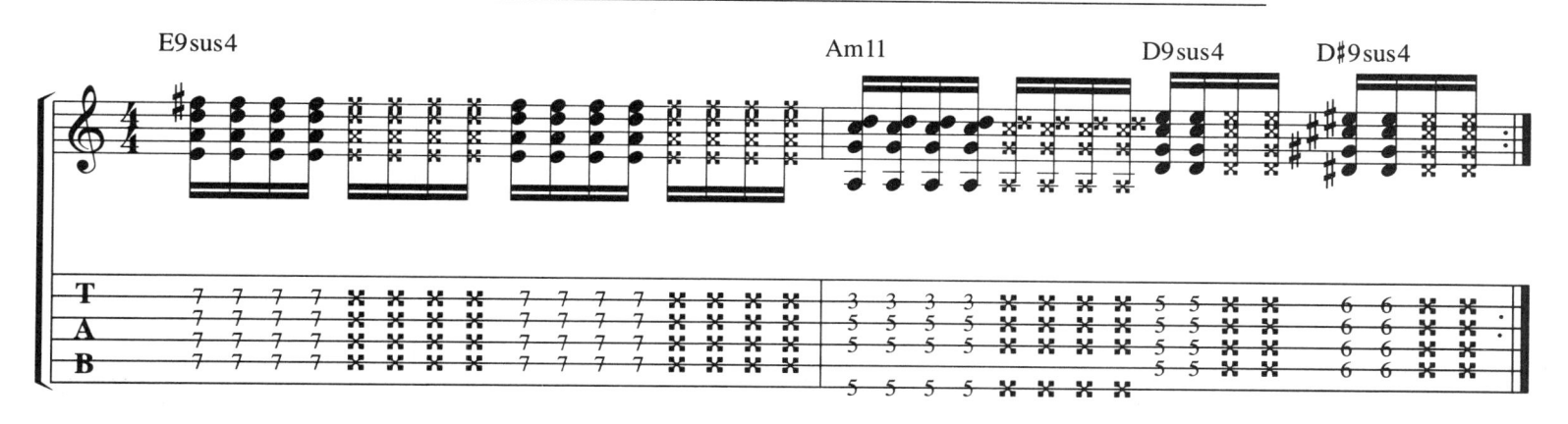

EXAMPLE 8

STEVE LUKATHER

In a groove setting, you don't want to be stepping on the keyboard player's left-hand part. You might want to find a little muted part that doesn't get in the way. The following figures use the E and D notes as common tones between the chords.

The notes in the E9sus4 chord are: E-B-D-F#-A
The notes in the Am11 chord are: A-C-E-G-B-D
The notes in the D9sus4 chord are: D-A-C-E-G
The notes in the D#9sus4 chord are: D#-A#-C#-E#-G#

Try playing Examples 9, 10, and 11 while someone else plays the foundation part.

EXAMPLE 9

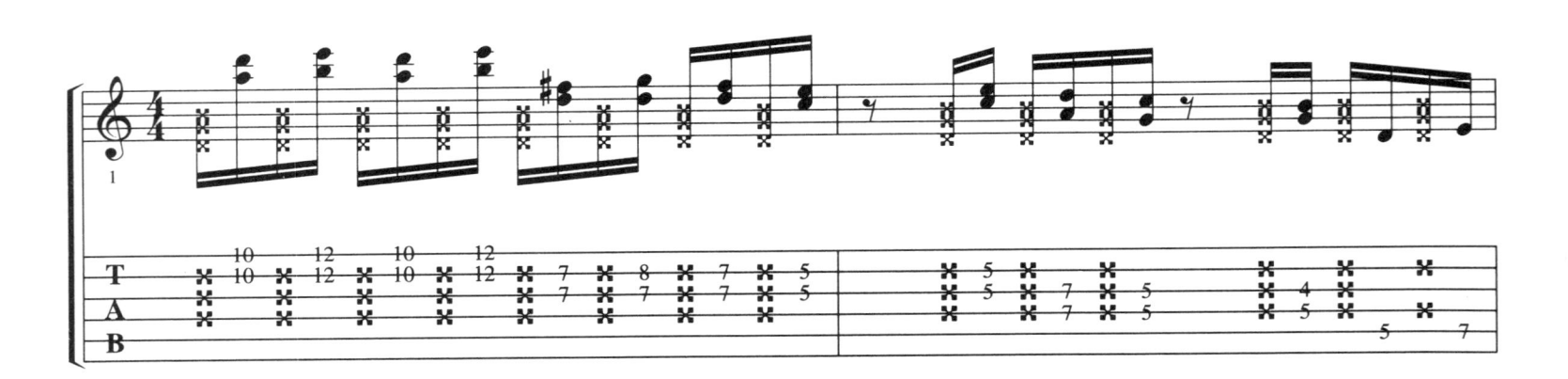

EXAMPLE 10

EXAMPLE 11

In Examples 12 and 13, this concept is applied to two other progressions.

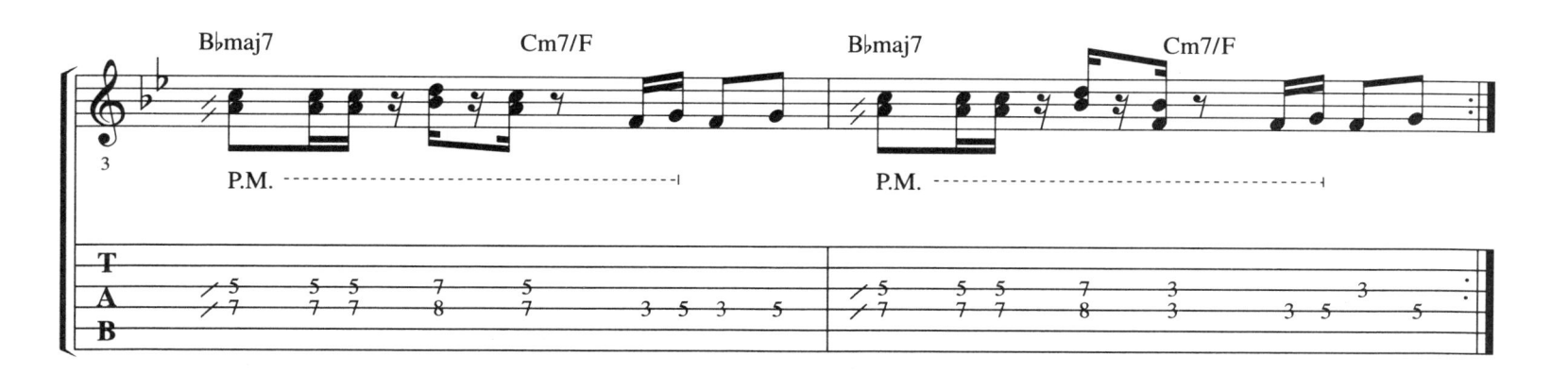

EXAMPLE 12

STEVE LUKATHER

Example 13

STEVE LUKATHER

The following is an excerpt from a song I play with my club band, Los Lobotomys. I think it's a good example of using jazz concepts while retaining a rock feel.

I hope you've found these pointers useful. Good luck and have fun!

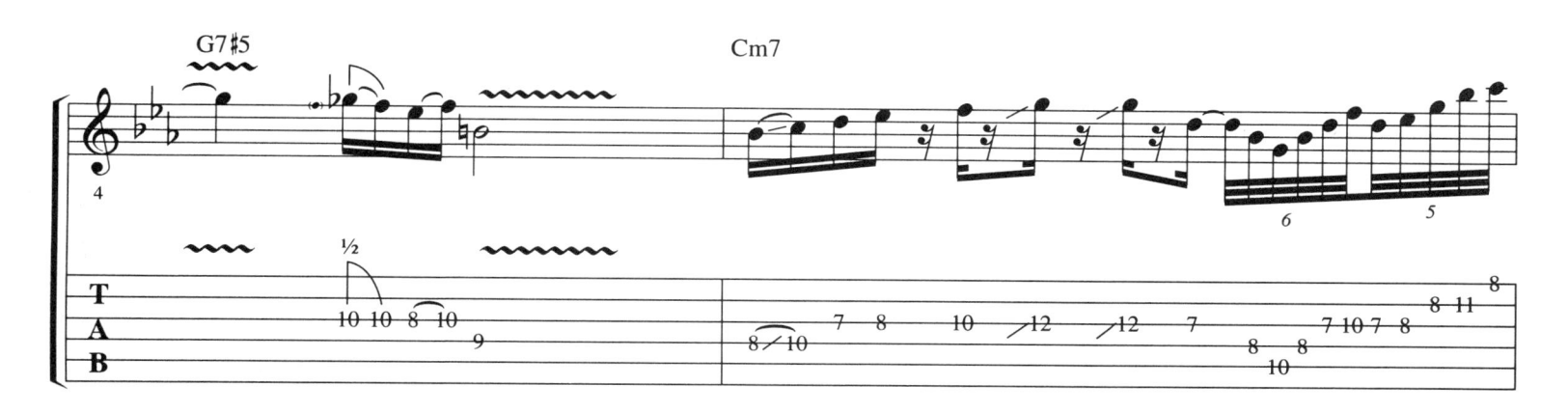

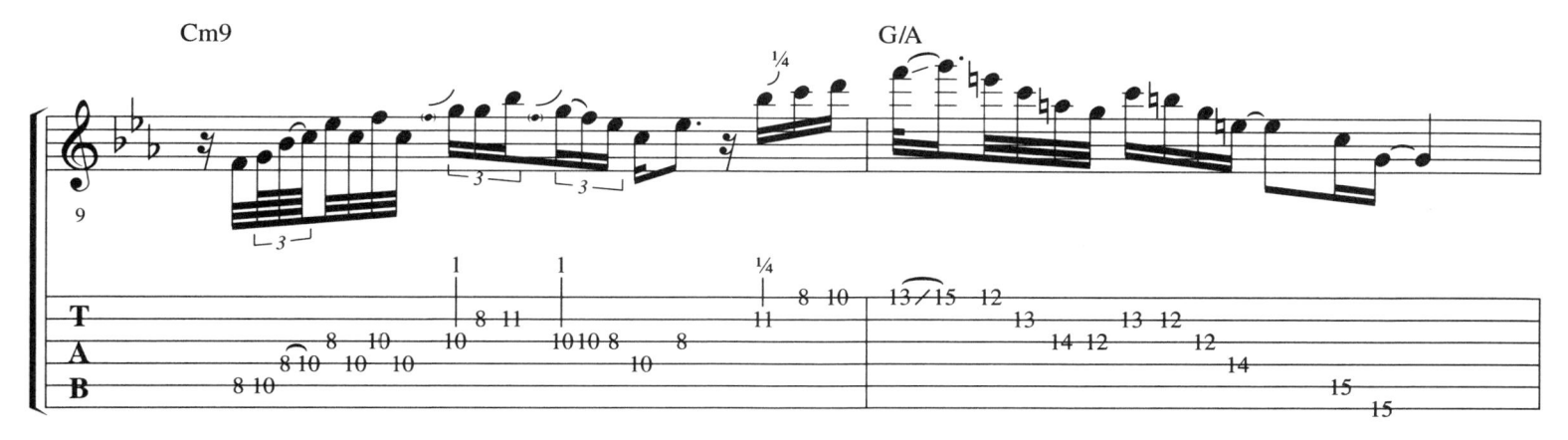

EXAMPLE 14

STEVE LUKATHER

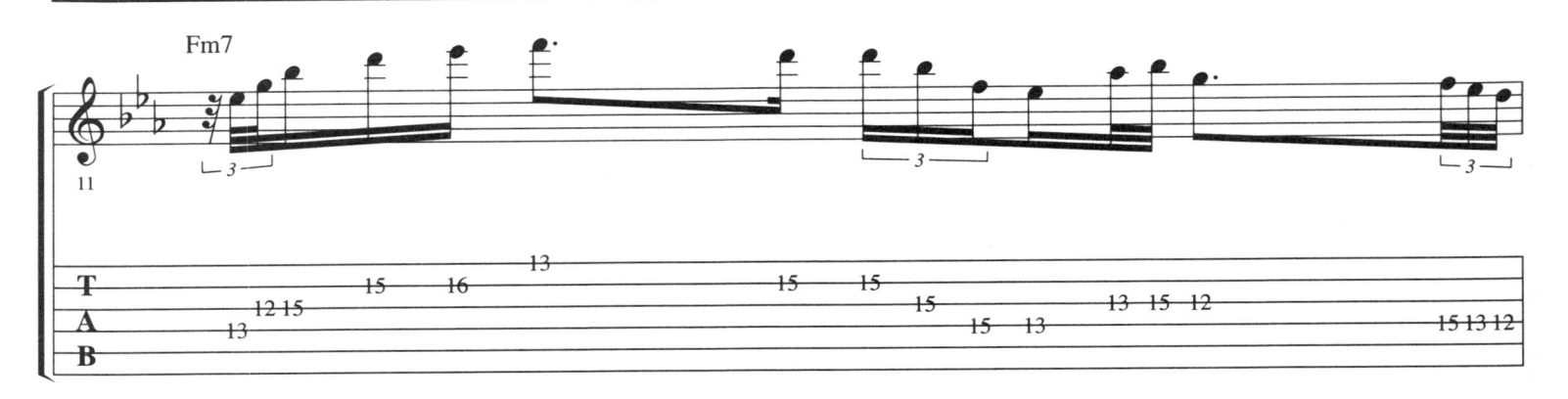

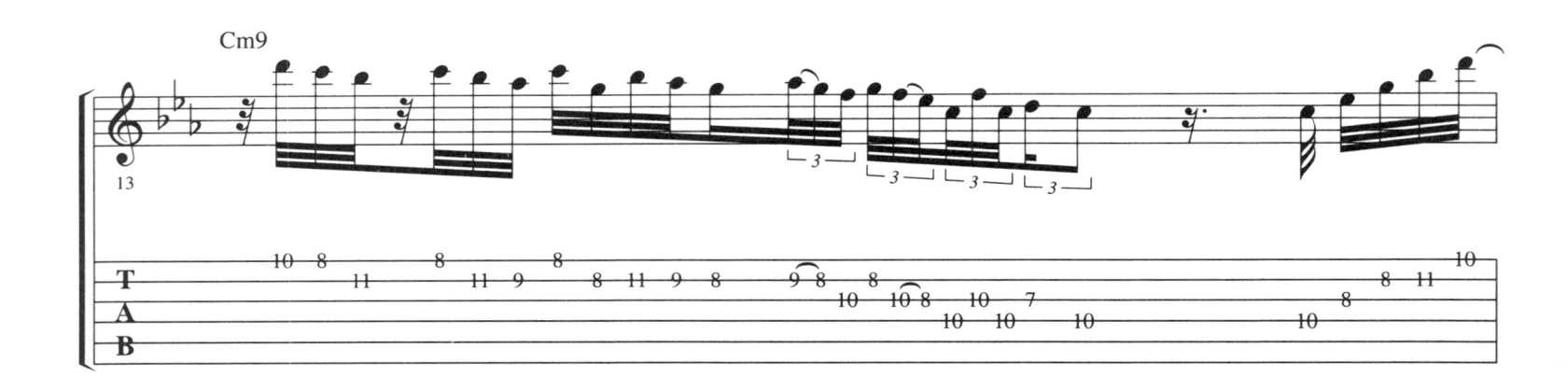

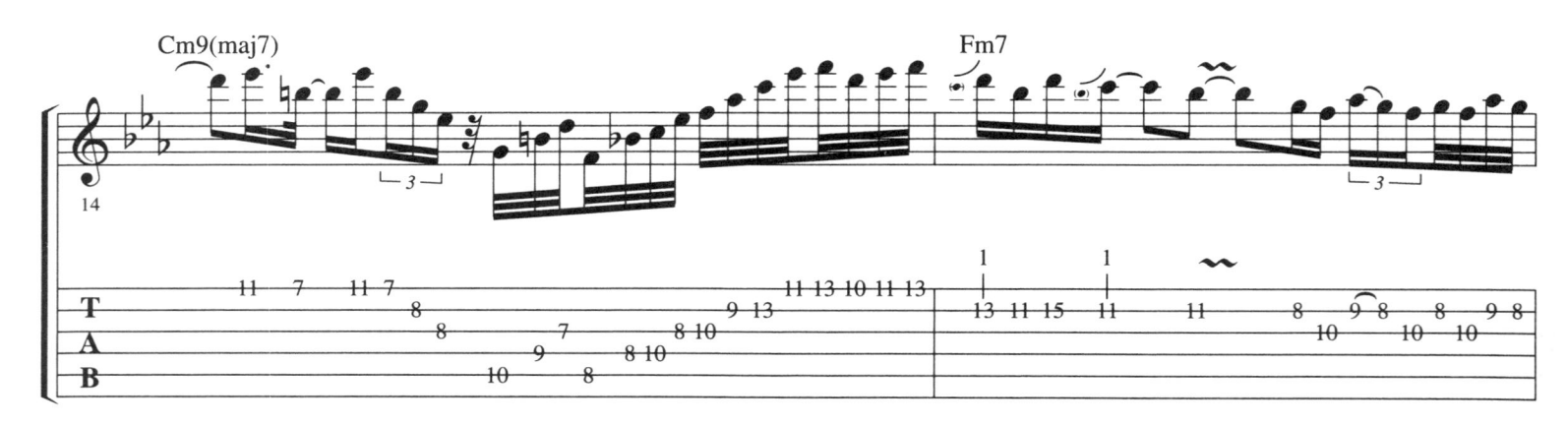

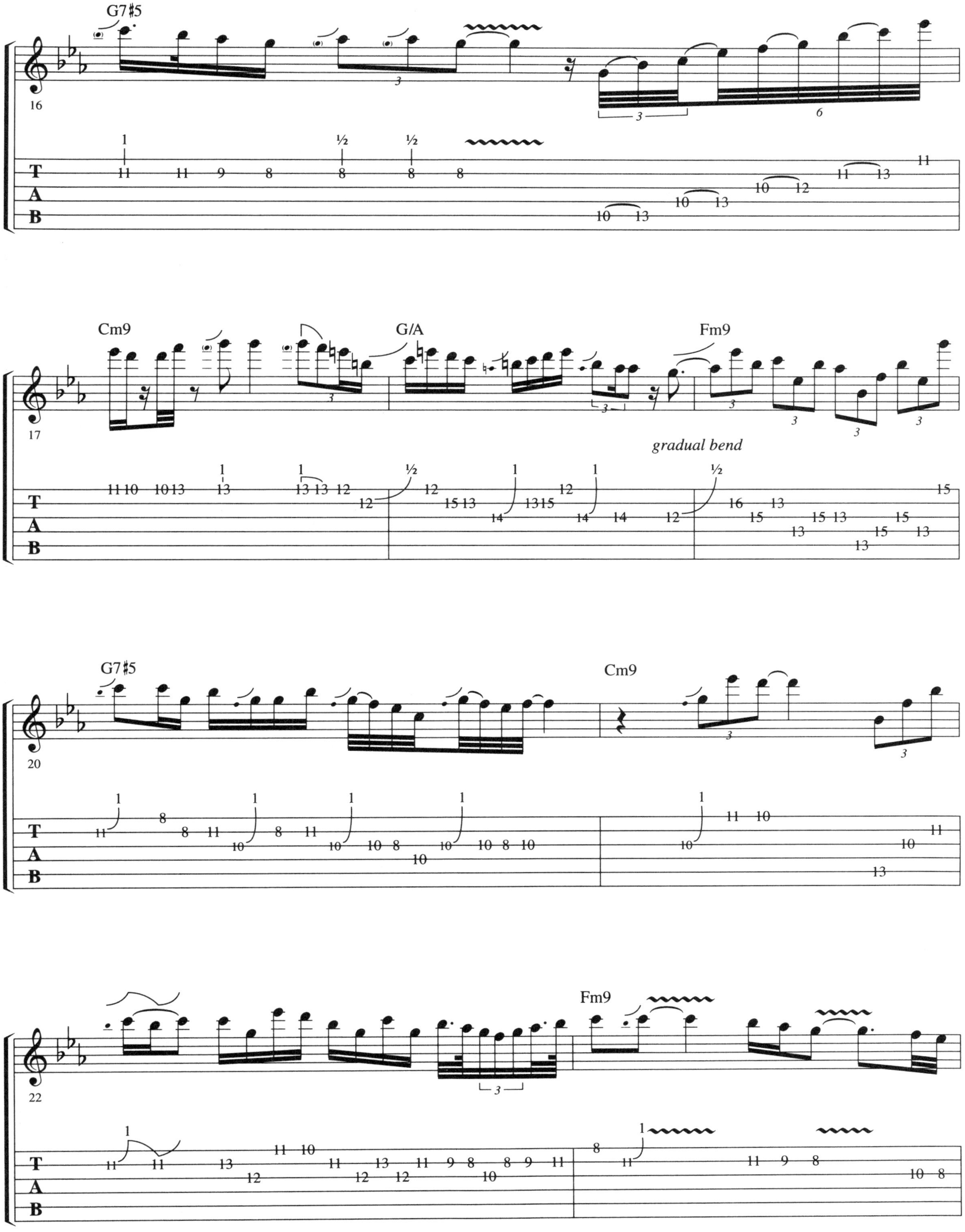
G7♯5
16
Cm9
G/A
Fm9
17
gradual bend
G7♯5
Cm9
20
22
Fm9

STEVE LUKATHER

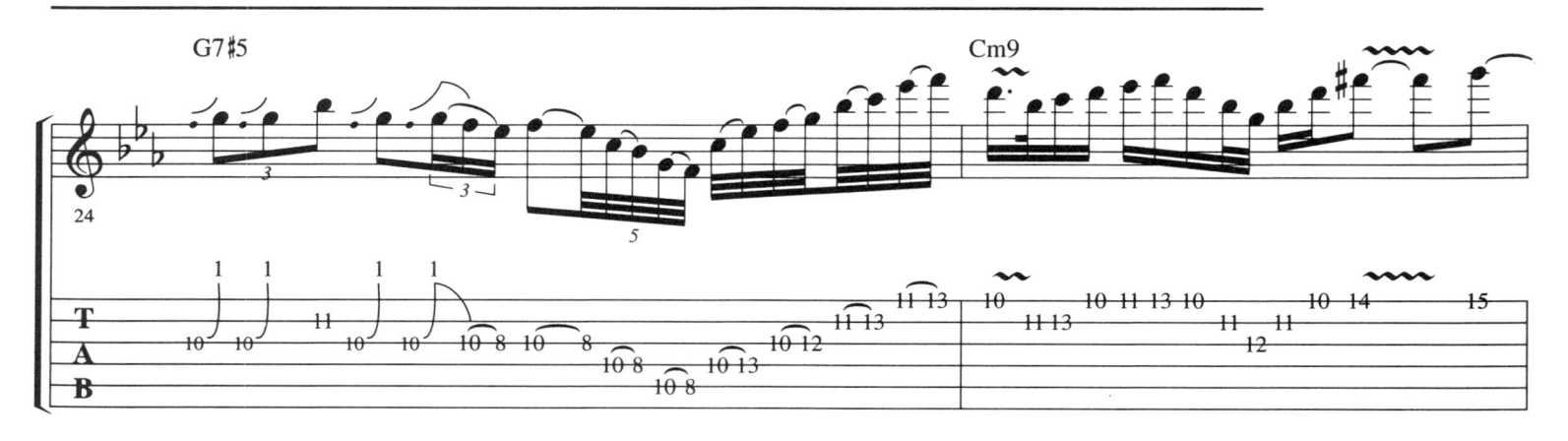

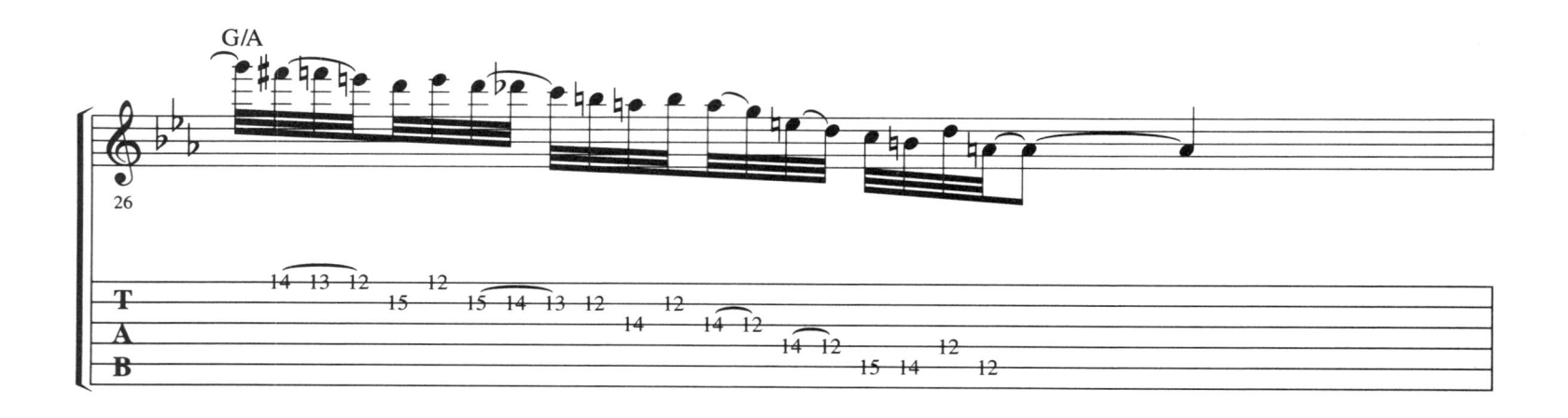

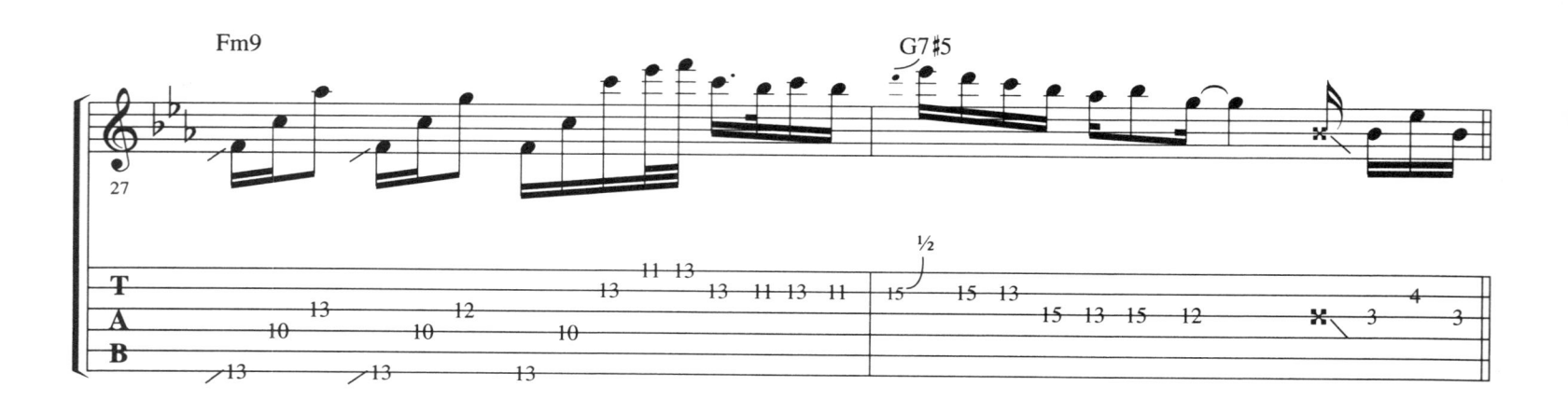

STEVE LUKATHER

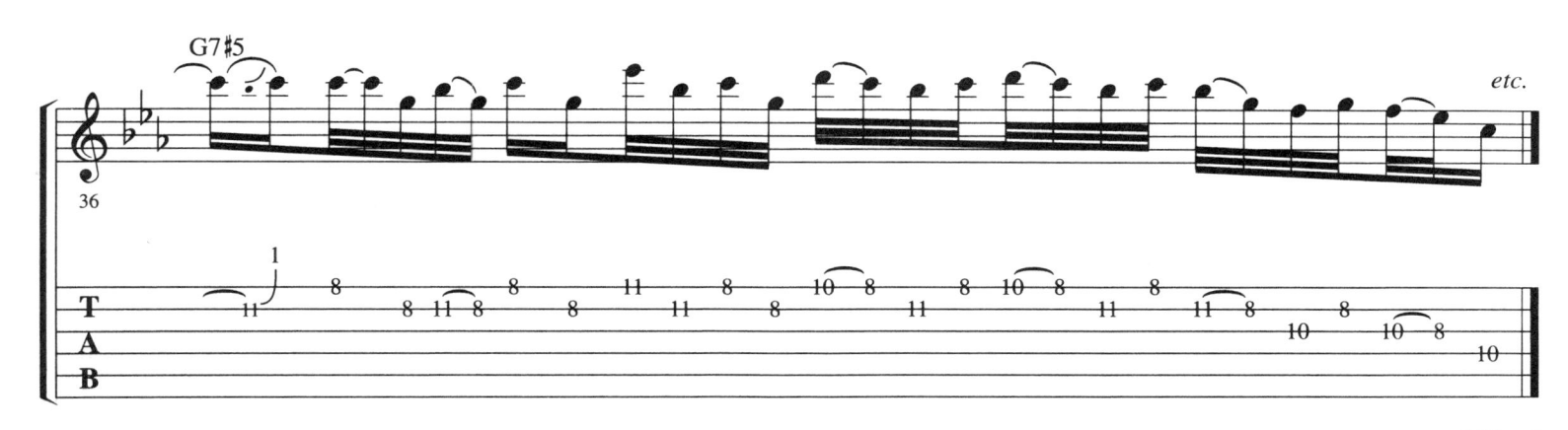

MIKE STERN

MIKE STERN WAS BORN IN 1953 IN BOSTON, AND BEGAN PLAYING guitar at age 12. "I liked the feel of it," he says "and I got hooked, but I didn't get serious until I went to Berklee in 1971." As a teenager, Stern was influenced by a wide range of artists including B.B. King, Jimi Hendrix, Eric Clapton, McCoy Tyner, John Coltrane, Sonny Rollins, "and, of course, Miles Davis." He also acknowledges a special debt to jazz guitar greats like Wes Montgomery and Jim Hall.

Mike attended the Berklee School of Music and studied with Pat Metheny and Mick Goodrick. In 1976, he recorded and toured with jazz/rock group Blood Sweat and Tears. Stern toured and recorded with the band for two years, appearing on their albums *More Than Ever* and *Brand New Day*.

Back in Boston, Stern continued his studies with renowned jazz pianist and teacher Charley Banacos, whom he credits with helping him develop a keen appreciation for straight-ahead jazz. In 1978, he joined drummer Billy Cobham's band. The following year, when the band played a series of dates at New York's Bottom Line, Miles Davis dropped in to hear Mike Stern. Miles obviously liked what he heard, and in 1981 offered Mike a spot in his band. "Miles was coming out of a self-imposed hiatus, and his return to the music scene took on the appearance of a media event," Mike recalls. "It was a tremendous opportunity. I absorbed a lot, learned a lot, and even now I'm still working on a lot of things he taught me." Stern left the band in 1983; two years later, Miles called and offered him the job again. Mike rejoined and worked with Davis for another year. During his three years with Miles Davis, he appeared on the albums *Man With The Horn*, *Star People*, and *We Want Miles*.

After his second stint with Miles ended, Mike spent a year with bassist Jaco Pastorius (his old friend) and another year "playing a lot of straight-ahead jazz gigs." His 1985 tour with alto saxophonist David Sanborn marked the beginning of a collaborative period during which he worked with Steps Ahead, the Michael Brecker Band, and a number of other respected musicians.

In 1989, Mike and Bob Berg formed the Mike Stern/Bob Berg Band with drummer Dennis Chambers and bassist Lincoln Goines. Acclaimed by critics and fans alike, they toured frequently in the U.S. and abroad. 1992 saw Stern touring and recording with the Brecker Brothers reunion band, as well as saxophone legend Joe Henderson's group. Currently, Mike tours mainly with his own trio, usually comprised of Lincoln Goines and drummer Ben Perowsky

Mike Stern has recorded six solo albums on Atlantic Records, including *Upside Downside*, *Time in Place*, *Jigsaw*, *Odds or Evens*, *Standards (and Other Songs)*, and his newest release, *Is What It Is*, which features, among others, Michael Brecker, Dennis Chambers, Will Lee, Jim Beard and Bob Malach.

In this chapter, Mike details his approach to playing standards and presents some of the techniques he uses to achieve the natural lyricism so evident in his playing.

(**Note:** All transcriptions, musical examples and fingerings interpreted by Mike Williams.)

MIKE STERN

LESSON 1 ▶ SOLOING OVER STANDARDS

Learning standards is an important part of one's musical development, no matter what style you choose to concentrate on; they are good vehicles for developing your soloing. Many of the great jazz artists include standards in their repertoire. If you want to learn some standard songs, I suggest listening to recordings by different artists. Each is sure to have a different "take" on the particular song. The new fake books contain listings of the best recorded versions of each tune. Don't listen only to the solos: pay careful attention to the way the melody is played. Most standards have very strong melodies often derived from chord tones. Chord tones (or arpeggios) are the notes of the chord.

This lesson will concentrate on the importance of chord tones in melodic playing. We'll use the major scale as our model and derive the chord tones from the following formulas. Let's take C major scale as an example: C-D-E-F-G-A-B-C.

The C major 7th (Cmaj7) arpeggio is the 1st, 3rd, 5th, and 7th.
The C minor 7th (Cm7) arpeggio is the 1st, ♭3rd, 5th, and ♭7th.
The C dominant 7th (C7) chord is the 1st, 3rd, 5th, and ♭7th.
The C diminished 7th chord is the 1st, ♭3rd, ♭5th, and ♭♭7th.
The C augmented 7th chord is the 1st, 3rd, ♯5th, and ♭7th.

ARPEGGIO SHAPES FOR THE GUITAR

The following are common two-octave arpeggio shapes. You'll be using these in this lesson, and in every type of music you play. I want to stress that it's very important to familiarize yourself with the arpeggios — but when improvising over a tape, try to avoid playing them as an exercise! If you get into the habit of playing arpeggios, your playing will sound too mechanical. Instead, use these notes as elements to create melodies.

Practice these in position and also on one string. When I practice the one-string arpeggios, I don't work on speed or a specific fingering; I practice for ear training and to develop my knowledge of the neck.

EXAMPLE 1

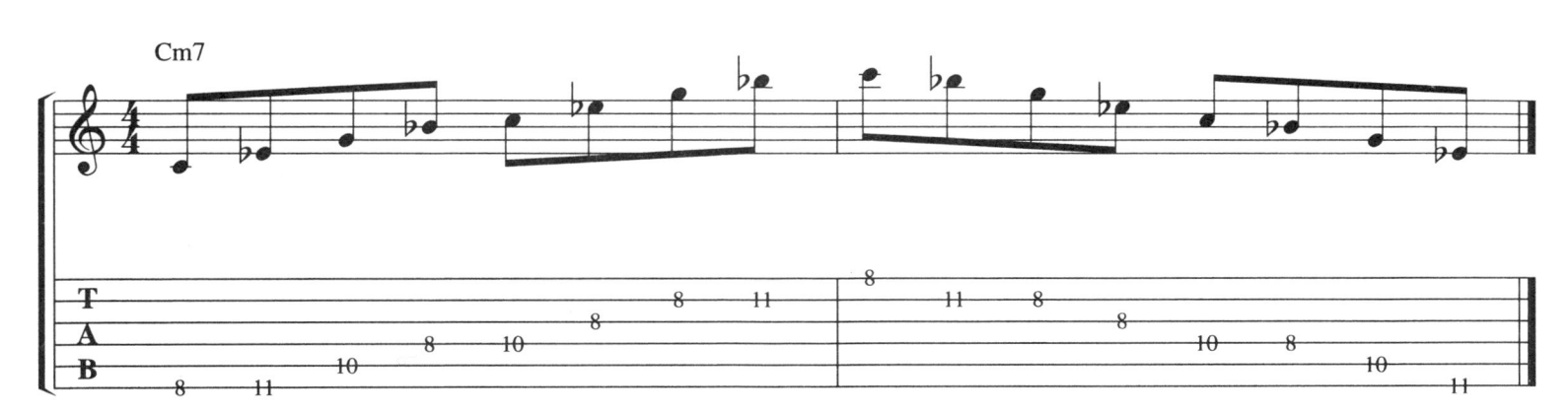

Mike Stern

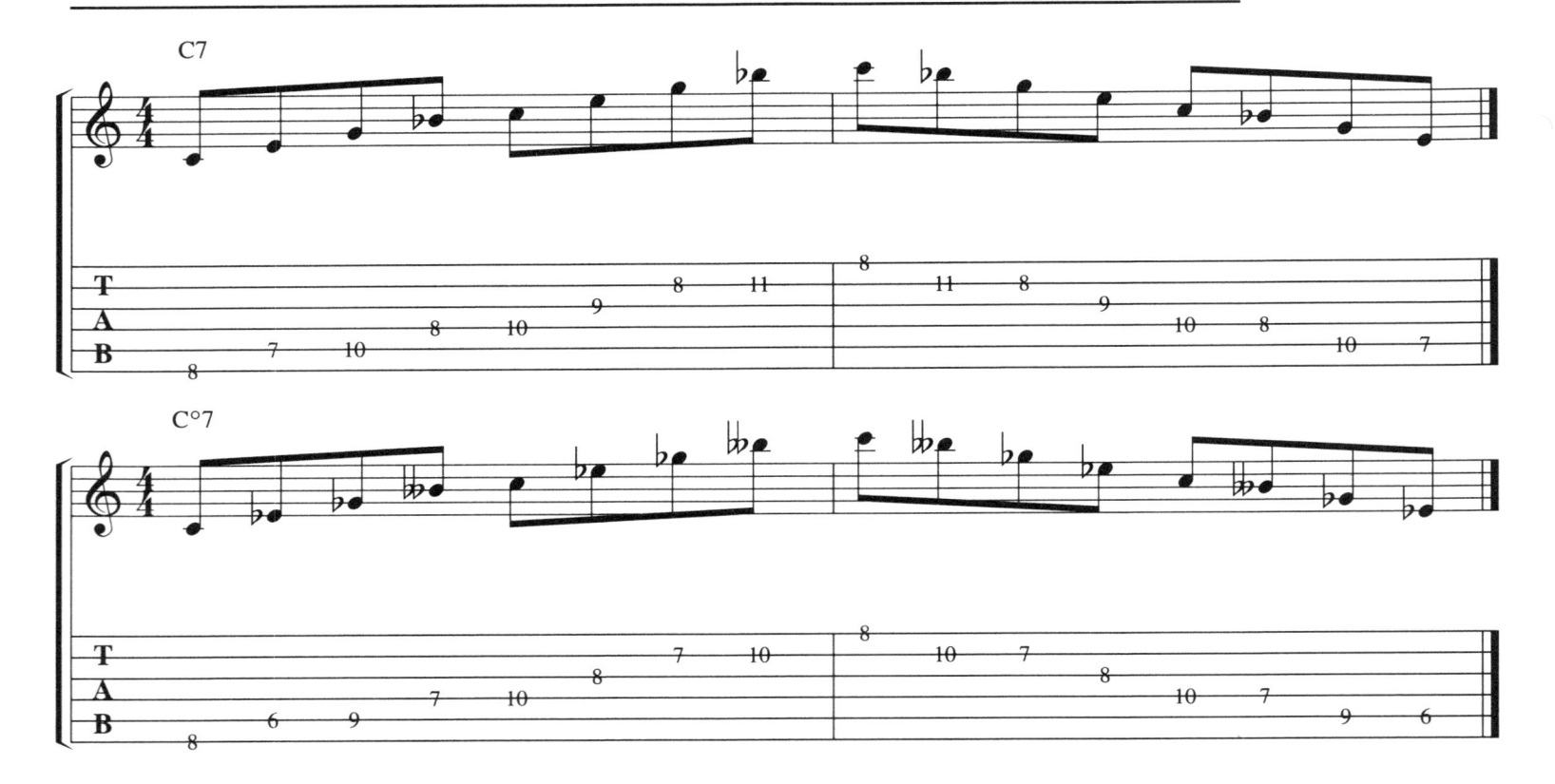

Soloing over Changes

Working on a standard is a good way to approach chord tone soloing. We're going to start with a familiar chord progression. If this is new to you, just take the first four measures. As we discussed, it's important to pay careful attention to melody.

Tape yourself playing the chords to the first four measures. Play them ten times through. If you use a metronome, set it at a slow swing tempo (around ♩=72 or slower); slowly enough that you can grasp it. Don't rush the learning process. It's important that your fingers don't go faster than your ears; you want to avoid relying on finger patterns.

Experiment with the following arpeggios as a basis for soloing using chord tones. You should probably familiarize yourself with these. I've written them as two octaves, but you can play one or three-octave arpeggios if you like. All octaves should be practiced, however.

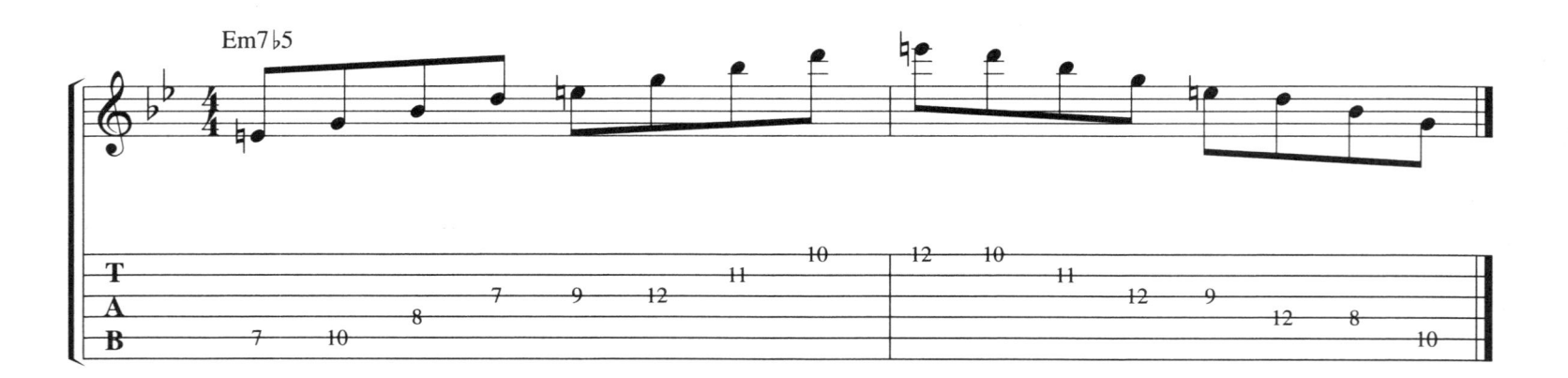

Example 2

MIKE STERN

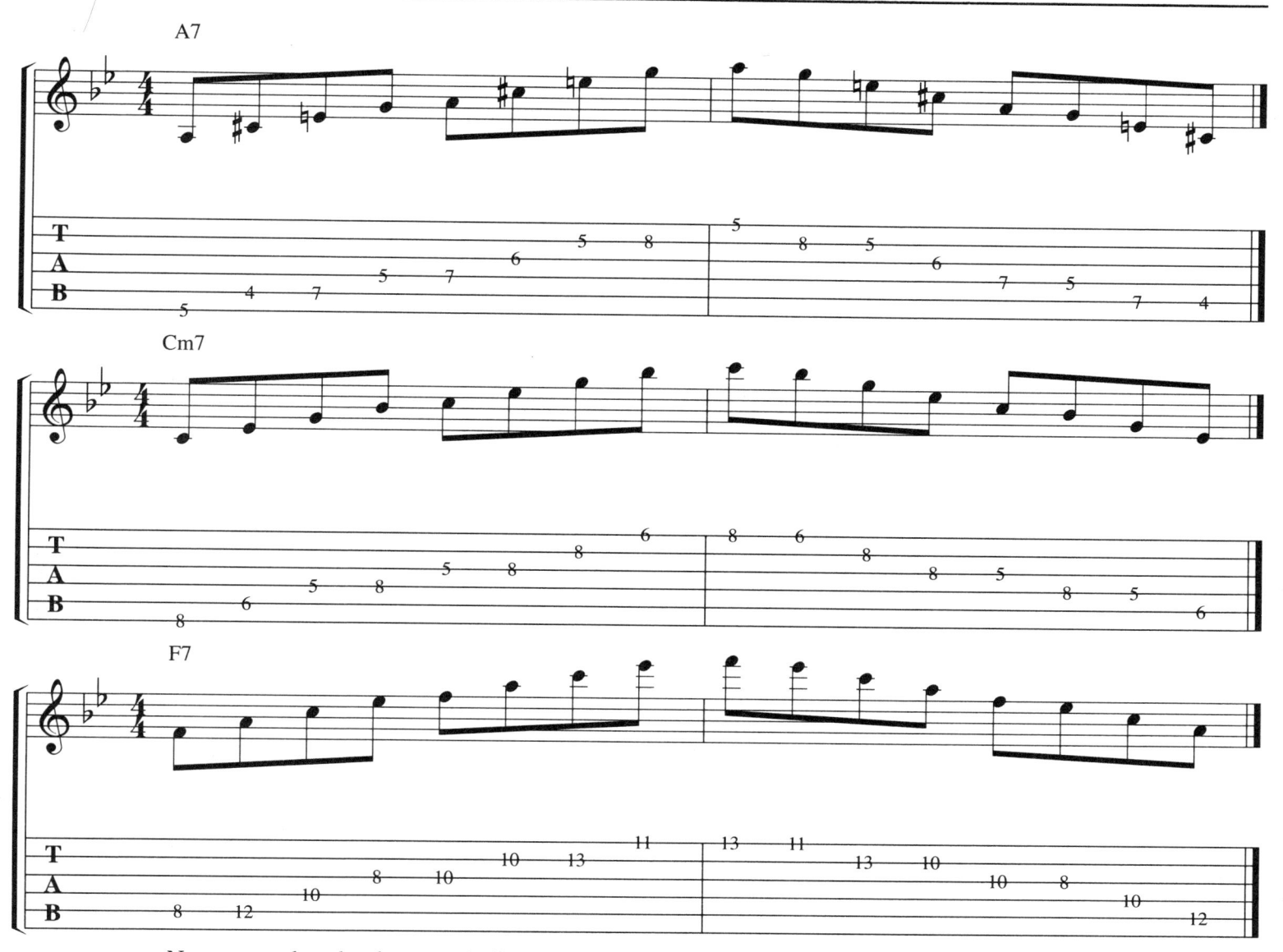

Now try to play chord tone melodies along with your practice tape. Once again, I want to stress that these are not to be played with your tape as an exercise. When you're improvising, you'll be using some or all of the chord tones to create melodies.

You can also practice the arpeggios in inversions. The following is an F major chord in root position, first inversion, second inversion, and third inversion. Using the formulas from the beginning of this lesson, alter them to form the four other chord types (dominant 7, minor 7, diminished 7 and augmented). Knowledge of the inversions will help you avoid playing the root as the first note of every measure. The more familiar you are with these formulas, the freer you'll be to make melodies; you will start hearing them. Now practice with your tape using some of your inversion knowledge.

EXAMPLE 3

Fmaj7 – root position

MIKE STERN

Fmaj7 – first inversion

Fmaj7 – second inversion

Fmaj7 – third inversion

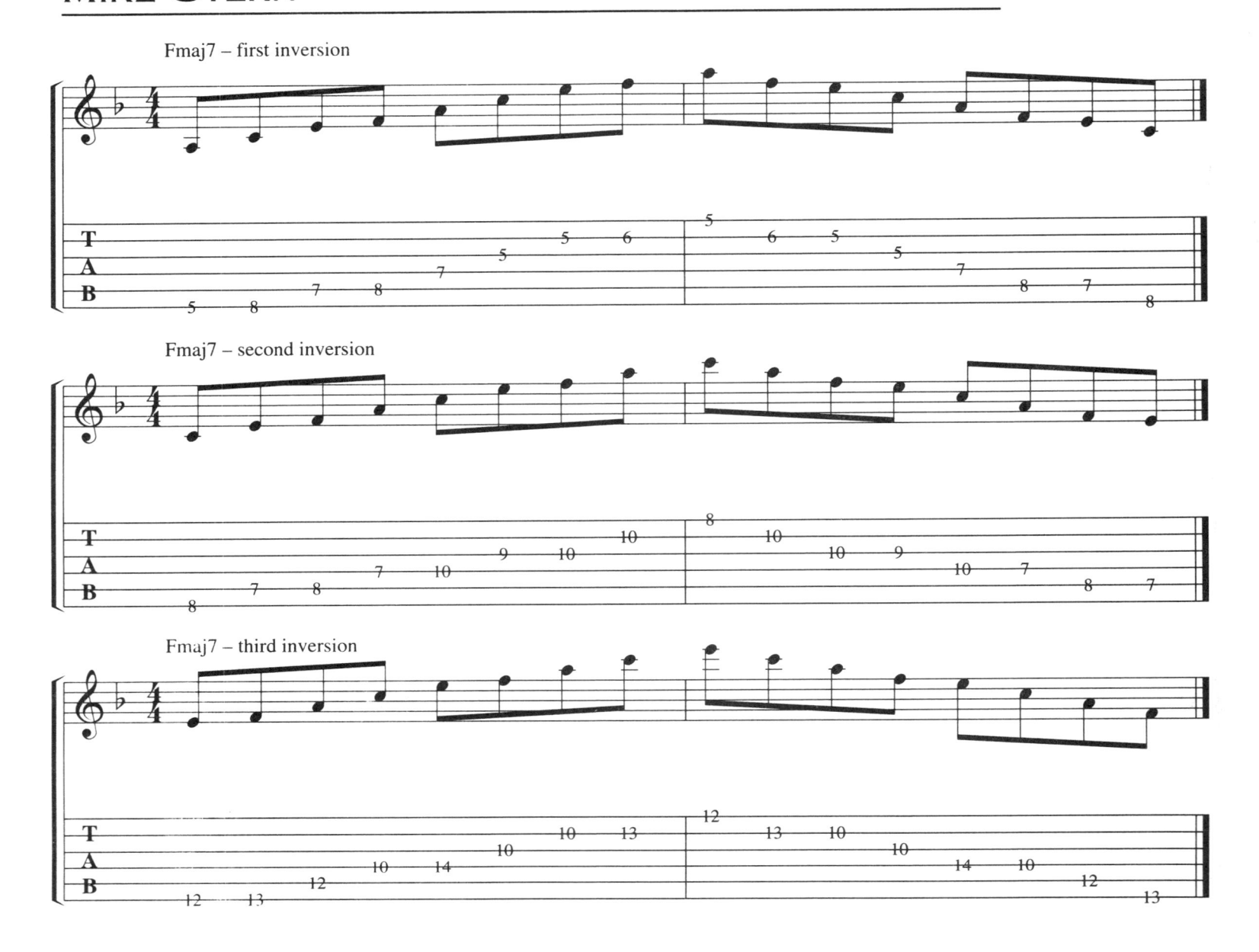

Following are my solos over a well-known chord progression as they appear on the accompanying CD (thanks to Bruce Whitcomb for his assistance with the recording). The first chorus of each solo consists mainly of chord tones. The second chorus is freed up a little, but I kept it pretty "inside" in order to illustrate the idea of chord tone melodies. You might try taping the chord changes and then playing this study with the tape. Then try your own!

EXAMPLE 4

Mike Stern

Mike Stern

Mike Stern

Mike Stern

EXAMPLE 5

Em7♭5
A7
Cm7
F7
Fm7
B♭7
E♭maj7
A♭7
B♭maj7
Em7♭5
A7
Dm7
B♭m7
E♭7
Fmaj7
Dm7
Gm7
C7
Am7♭5
D7
G7alt.
Cm7
T
A
B

Mike Stern

Mike Stern

Mike Stern

LESSON 2 ▶ MAPPING OUT TONAL CENTERS

Another way of soloing over changes is to loop them all together in "tonal centers" or "key centers." If we analyze the first four measures of our progression, we find that the first two measures are in D minor, and the next two bars are a ii7-V7 in B♭ major. By mapping out the tonal centers, it becomes easy to add scaler lines to your chord tone solos. Using the tonal centers indicated, try adding the scales while soloing over the following.

Playing over changes is a skill that is not learned quickly. If you're having difficulty, don't feel alone: when I first started soloing over changes, I felt very shy and awkward. It took me a long time to feel comfortable. It takes a lot of work but the rewards are worth the effort.

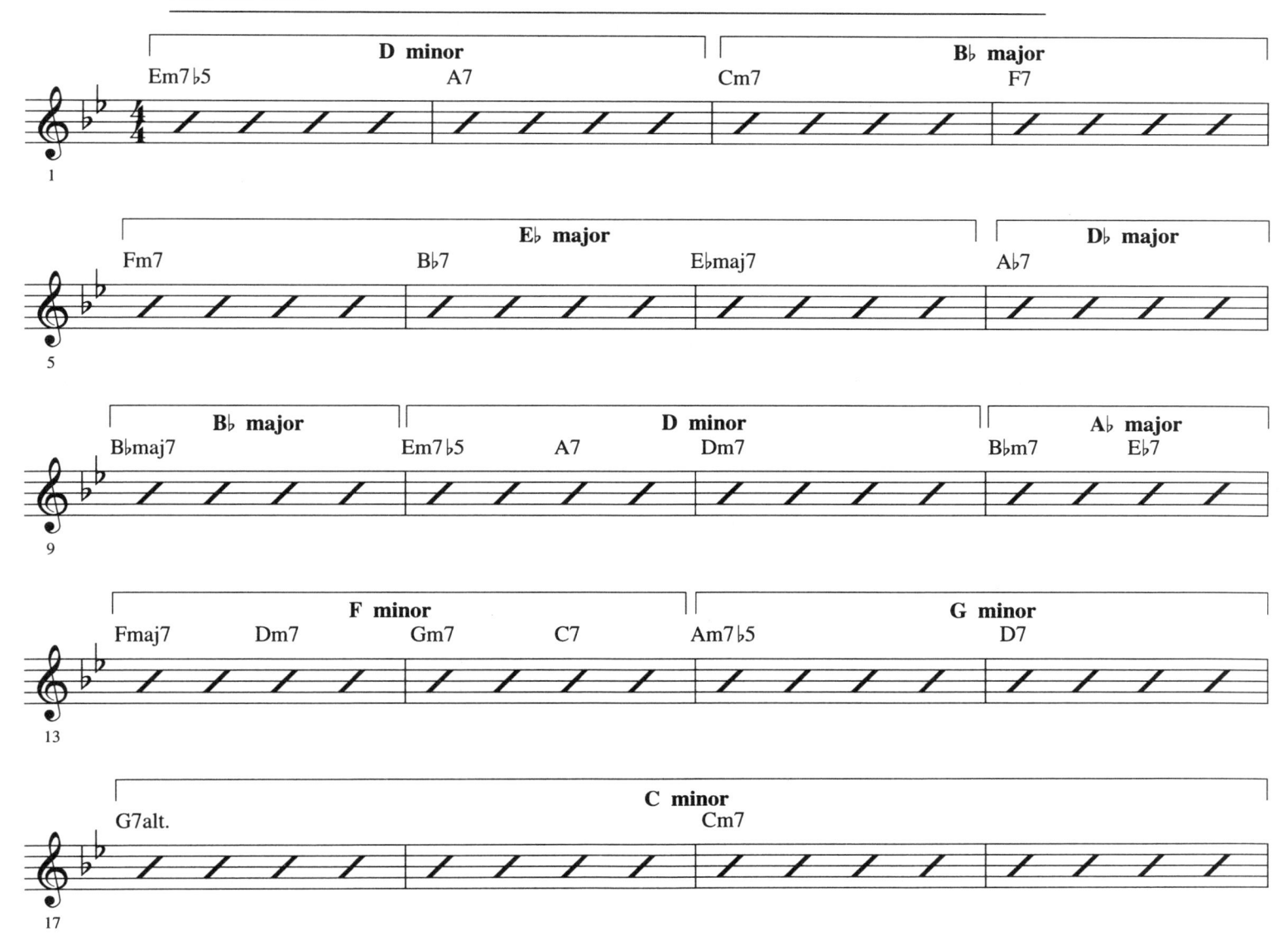

EXAMPLE 6

Mike Stern

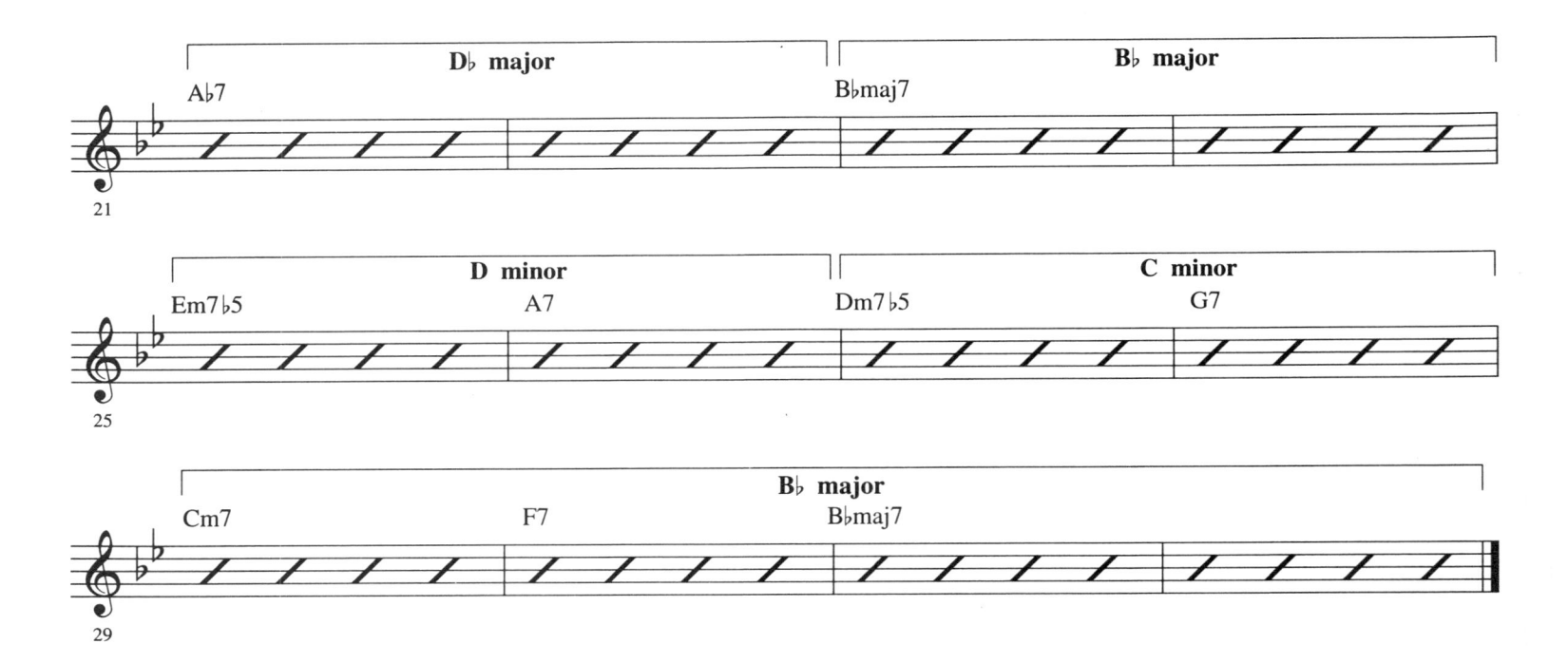

```
        Db major                              Bb major
Ab7                     Bbmaj7
(measures 21-24: slash notation)

        D minor                               C minor
Em7b5                   A7        Dm7b5       G7
(measures 25-28: slash notation)

                        Bb major
Cm7          F7         Bbmaj7
(measures 29-32: slash notation)
```

Lesson 3 ▶ Listening

My soloing style has definitely been influenced by other players. Although I listen to other guitarists, the majority of my practice time was (and still is) spent checking out horn and piano players. My style evolved from my pursuit of a horn-like sound and style. I try to avoid memorizing figures or licks, since this would detract from the freshness and spontaneity I strive for in my playing. Although I've studied many styles and players, I've never actually memorized any one person's playing. The idea is not to try to copy someone else's style; but by listening closely to players you admire, and sometimes transcribing their solos, you'll find their phrasing comes out naturally in your playing.

It's important to learn about the musicians who have come before us and to study their musical vocabulary. Once you've done this, you can put your own stamp on the music and make up new "words." Learning music is similar to learning a language. First you learn words. Then the words become sentences. Sentences become paragraphs, and with paragraphs you can tell a story.

Written transcription is essential to this study method. While transcription can be difficult, its positive impact on your soloing will make it worthwhile. By writing down other players' lines instead of memorizing them, you're more likely to sound influenced rather than cloned. By the way, you may find a tape recorder with a half-speed function useful in transcribing certain solos.

I'd like to mention two recordings that especially influenced me: John Coltrane's "Live at the Village Vanguard" (Impulse, 1962) and Dizzy Gillespie's "The Eternal Triangle," with Sonny Rollins and Sonny Stitt (Verve, 1958). I highly recommend listening to them and transcribing one solo from each. Then read through your transcriptions, but don't memorize them note for note. When it's time to play a gig, try to let go and allow your instincts to take over. The goal of improvisation, after all, is spontaneity.

"The Eternal Triangle" is based on the changes in the standard tune "I Got Rhythm." The following are transcriptions of some of the lines that Sonny Stitt uses against the first four measures of the A section. Since so many jazz tunes are based on this chord progression, reworking some of these ideas on guitar has really helped me develop my style. Once you record the chord progression, play the figures along with your tape.

Mike Stern

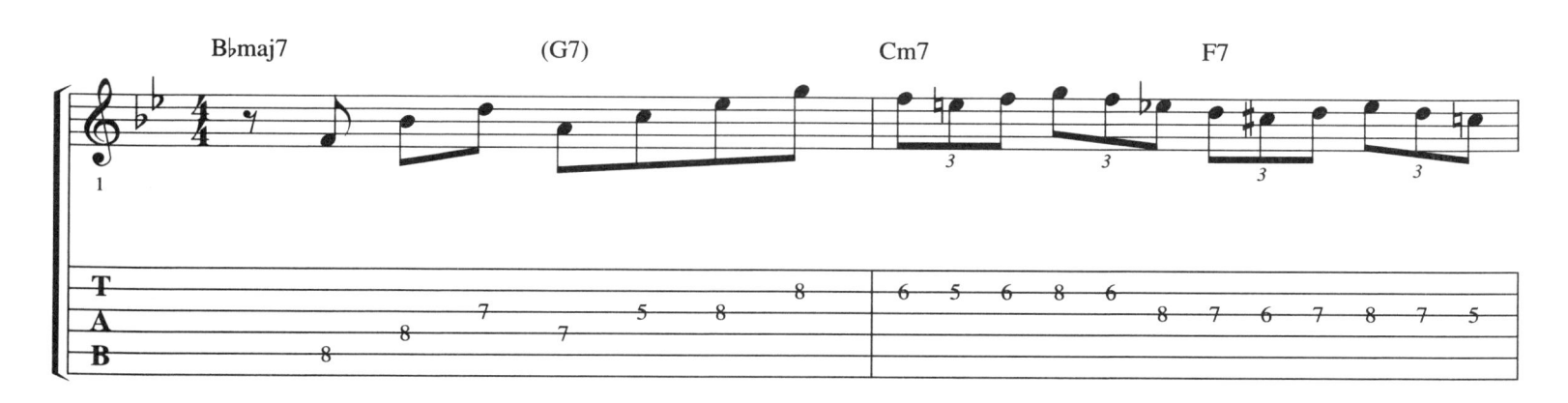

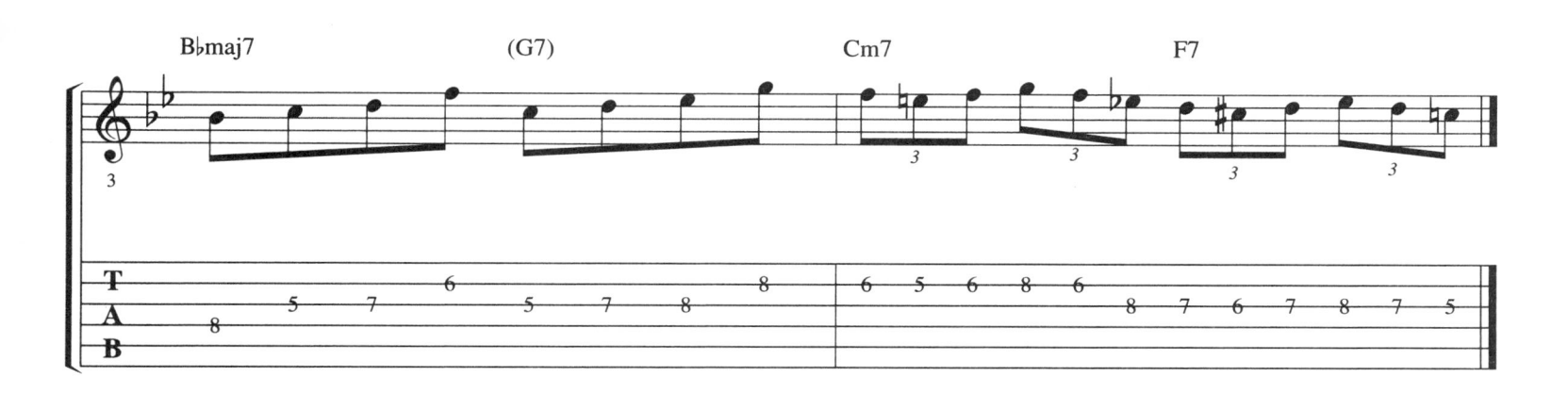

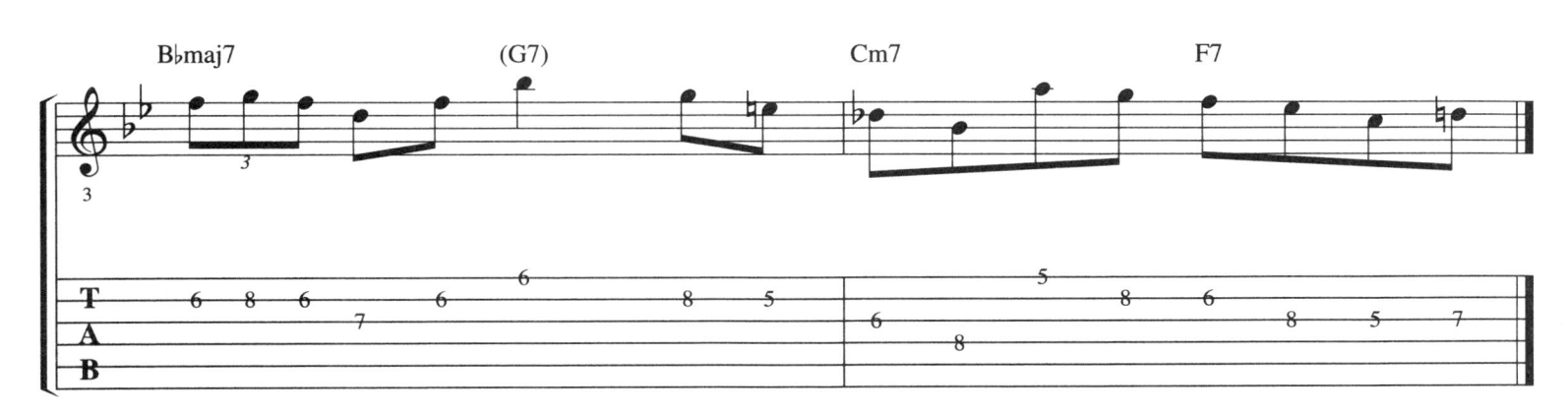

Example 7

Mike Stern

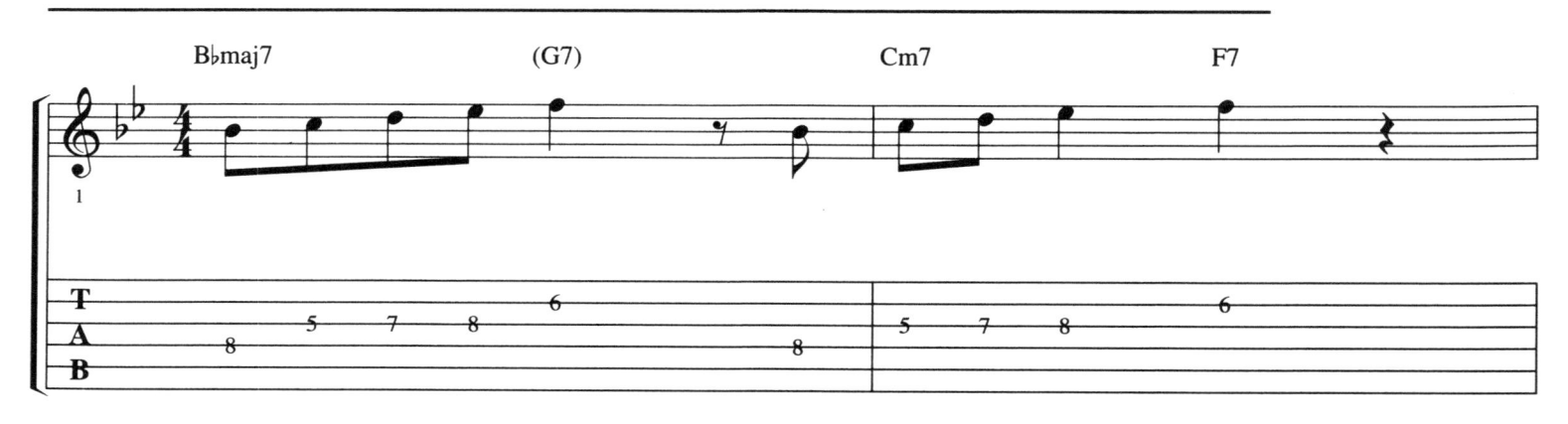

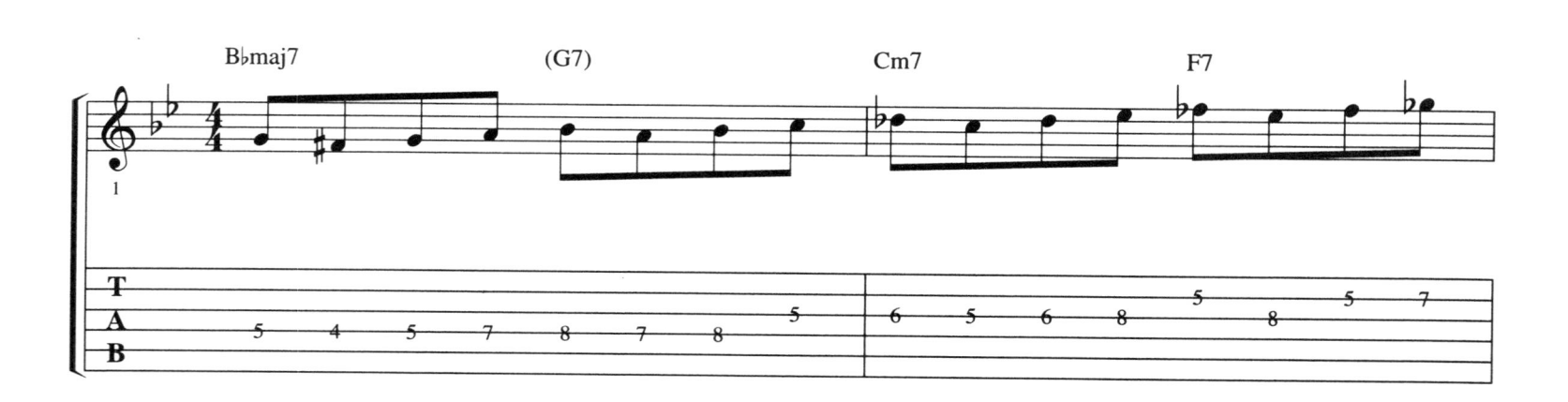

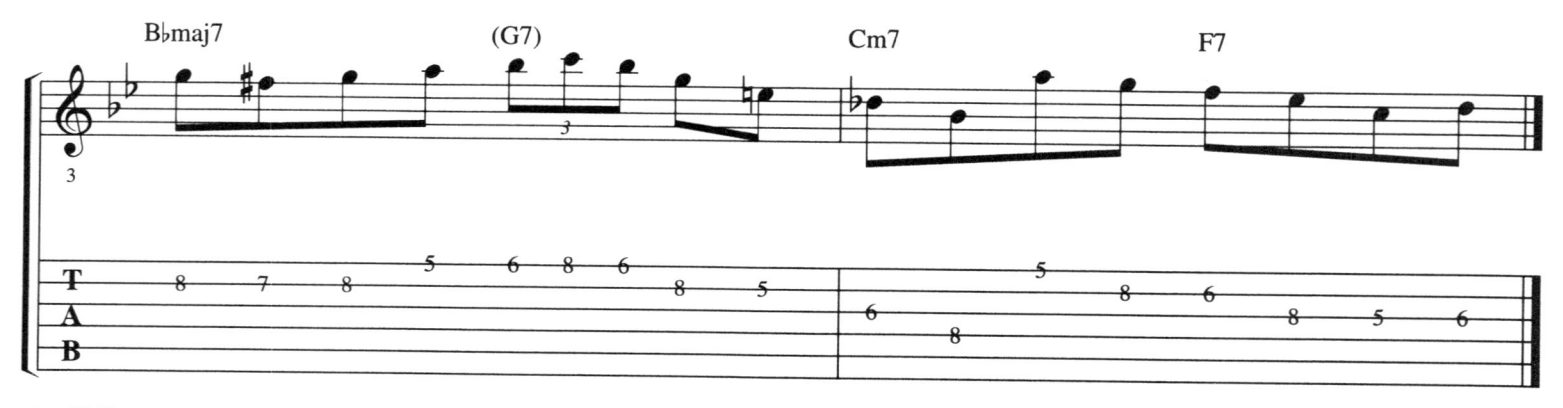

Mike Stern

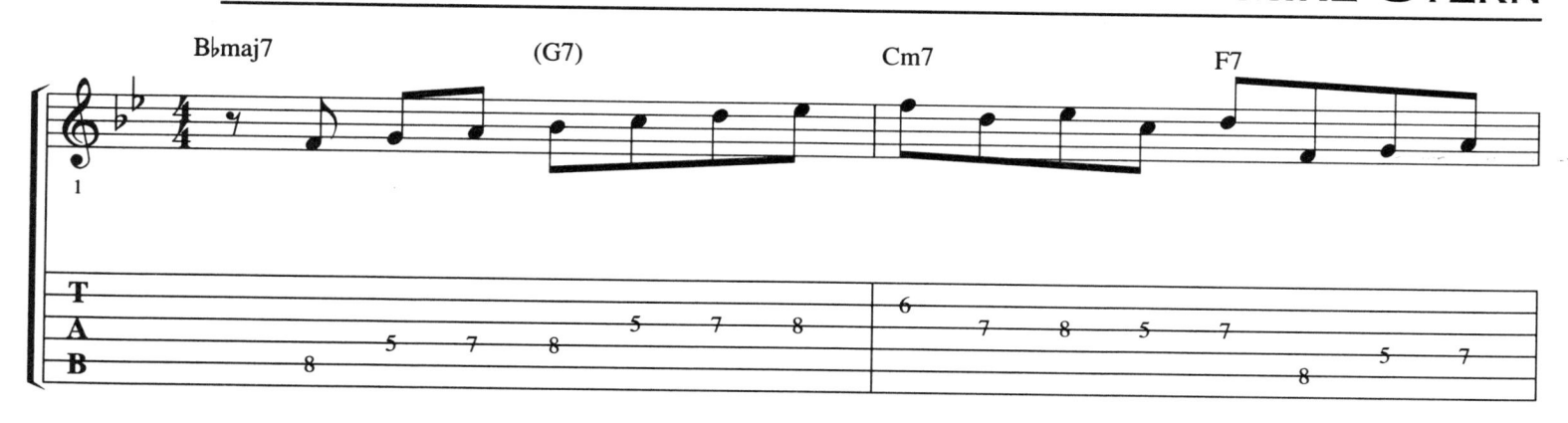

Mike Stern

Lesson 4 ▶ Soloing over a Static Chord

In this lesson we're going to explore a few of the many ways to approach soloing over a static chord.

Keep in mind as we proceed with this lesson that you are attempting to "speak a new language." Every time you discover a new option, it's like learning a new "word." You need to store each new idea in your overall musical vocabulary. It's important for all of us to learn slowly and to absorb each new idea thoroughly. Don't try to take shortcuts. Eventually you won't need to think about these concepts consciously, and in the end, they'll flow more naturally and your solos won't sound "thought out."

Following is an excerpt from my solo in "Gossip." The **A** section of this tune is loosely based on the **A symmetrical diminished** scale. The notes in the A symmetrical diminished scale are:

A-B♭-C-C♯-D♯-E-F♯-G

The excerpt from my solo contains elements of the A symmetrical diminished scale. Analyze which notes suggest this scale. Notice that it contains the ♭9, ♯9, ♭7, ♯11, and ♮13. These alterations provide the player with some tension notes that may help develop his or her solo. The following is a fifth position fingering that I use.

Example 8

MIKE STERN

The following examples are symmetrical diminished patterns. These will help you become familiar with the sound of this type of pattern. Record the chord and practice playing these patterns along with your tape. Experiment. Write your own lines. Listen to how others might use this scale, and eventually you'll be able to put the scale to use more easily to express your own ideas.

While a lesson like this is useful, remember that listening and playing are ultimately the most important learning tools. As soon as you feel ready, you should be playing with other musicians. Before that, a recorded music-minus-one situation can be very helpful.

I think one should listen on an analytical and, more importantly, on an emotional level. It's easy to get lost in the intellectual side of music. Don't forget that, as corny as it may sound, music is a means to express emotions. Playing from the heart is what counts.

EXAMPLE 9

Mike Stern

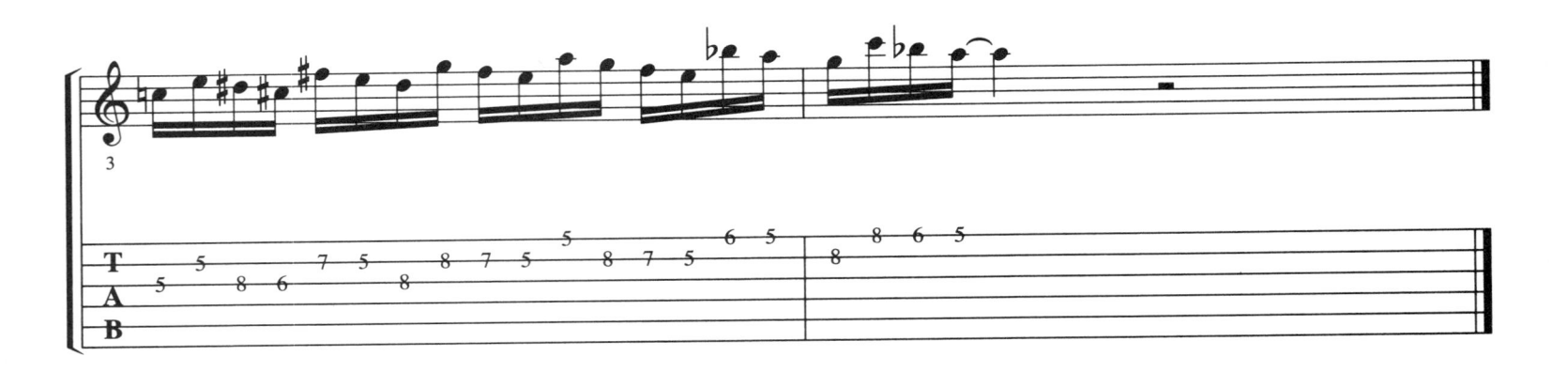

ABOUT THE CO-AUTHOR

MIKE WILLIAMS HAS BEEN A PROFESSIONAL musician for the past 25 years. As a classical guitar performance major at Cal State Hayward, he maintained a busy performance schedule, and continues today with concerts, club work, recording and solo recitals.

Mike began teaching privately in 1972. Many of his students have won scholarships to such prestigious schools as the New England Conservatory of Music, University of Redlands, Berkeley and USC. He has also taught Guitar and Music Literature courses since 1987 at Los Medanos College. Mike serves as an adjudicator in San Francisco Bay Area high school and college band competitions and works as an instructor at various summer music camps.

A Selected List of Books and Videos Available from CPP Media Group

Books/Audio Packages

Robben Ford
The Blues and Beyond
Playin' The Blues

Frank Gambale
Technique Book I
Technique Book II

Paul Gilbert
Intense Rock II

B.B. King
BluesMaster I
BluesMaster II
BluesMaster III
BluesMaster Complete

Yngwie Malmsteen
Yngwie Malmsteen

Steve Morse
Complete Styles
Essential Steve Morse

John Scofield
Jazz Funk Guitar I
Jazz Funk Guitar II

Videos

Frank Gambale
Monster Licks & Speed Picking
Modes: No More Mystery

Scott Henderson
Jazz Fusion Improvisation
Melodic Phrasing

John Scofield
Jazz Funk Guitar I
Jazz Funk Guitar II
Jazz Funk Guitar Box Set

Herb Ellis
Swing Jazz Soloing & Comping

Albert Lee
Advanced Country Guitar
Virtuoso Technique

Shawn Lane
Power Licks
Power Solos

Pat Martino
Creative Force Part I
Creative Force Part II

Steve Morse
Complete Styles of Steve Morse
Essential Steve Morse

Marty Friedman
Melodic Control

Allan Holdsworth
Allan Holdsworth

For Information and a Free Catalog contact:

CPP Media Group
15800 N.W. 48th Avenue
Miami, FL 33014
1-800-628-1528